THE Ś[illegible]

THE ŚRĀDDHA

THE HINDU BOOK OF THE DEAD

A Treatise on the
Śrāddha Ceremonies

Translated by
R.C. PRASAD

MOTILAL BANARSIDASS PUBLISHERS
PRIVATE LIMITED • DELHI

First Edition: Delhi, 1995
Reprint: Delhi, 1997

ISBN: 81-208-1192-5

MOTILAL BANARSIDASS

41 U.A. Bungalow Road, Jawahar Nagar, Delhi 110 007
8, Mahalaxmi Chamber, Warden Road, Mumbai 400 026
120 Royapettah High Road, Mylapore, Chennai 600 004
Sanas Plaza, Subhash Nagar, Pune 411 002
16 St. Mark's Road, Bangalore 560 001
8 Camac Street, Calcutta 700 017
Ashok Rajpath, Patna 800 004
Chowk, Varanasi 221 001

PRINTED IN INDIA

BY JAINENDRA PRAKASH JAIN AT SHRI JAINENDRA PRESS,
A-45 NARAINA, PHASE I, NEW DELHI 110 028
AND PUBLISHED BY NARENDRA PRAKASH JAIN FOR
MOTILAL BANARSIDASS PUBLISHERS PRIVATE LIMITED,
BUNGALOW ROAD, DELHI 110 007

Dedicated
to
Yama, Grahas and the Pitṛs
to
Propitiate whom the Obsequial
Rites are Performed

CONTENTS

Preface

In offering this book to the purohitas and householders our intention is not to rival the Books of the Dead, the Tibetan and the Egyptian. In the 'Commentary' on *The Tibetan Book of the Dead,* Chögyam Trungpa communicates 'the message of the book' in the following words:

> There seems to be a fundamental problem when we refer to the subject of *The Tibetan Book of the Dead.* The approach of comparing it with *The Egyptian Book of the Dead* in terms of mythology and lore of the dead person seems to miss the point, which is the fundamental principle of birth and death recurring constantly in this life. One could refer to this book as "The Tibetan Book of Birth". The book is not based on death as such, but on a completely different concept of death. It is a "Book of Space". Space contains birth and death; space creates the environment in which to behave, breathe and act; it is the fundamental environment which provides the inspiration for this book.

Our approach to the dead is not that of a non-dualist; the Advaitavādin's tendency to look upon births and deaths as an identical phenomenon, the one giving birth to the other, is not practicable on the terrestrial plane by a common householder to whom death is death, the loss of a person's life. To a common householder such ideas as 'Death is the soul's liberation from the prison-house of the body', 'Death is casting off worn-out bodies and entering into others which are new', 'Birth and death apply to everybody constantly, at this very moment', etc. hardly console one left behind by a dead person. Our daily living situation refuses to believe that the dead will ever return or that death is a renewal of life. We treat the dead as dead and, inspired by a sense of gratitude, pay whatever homage and largesse we can afford. Elaborate rituals, which include prayers for the peace of the deceased and offerings of material objects for use by the disembodied soul, are recommended by the dharmaśāstra.

It is not surprising, therefore, that the 'Hindu Book of the Dead', like the Tibetan, opens with the kinsfolk surrounding the person on death-bed and chanting inspiration-prayer calling on the Lord for rescue. *The Tibetan Book of the Dead* insists that 'at the time of one's death, one should always call on the Buddhas and the Bodhisattvas for rescue. One should make material and mental offerings to the Three Jewels, and holding fragrant incense in one's hand, say these words with intense power of concentration.' The kinsfolk of the dying Hindu do not belittle the importance of this simple ritual and recite scriptural texts and sing bhajanas. In most cases, when the dying man grows faint with fear, terror and bewilderment, the hymns are sung, episodes from the epics recounted, and sūktis from the śāstras read. The purpose of all this is not only to fill the dying with fortitude but also to remind him that 'now what is called death has arrived. You are not alone in leaving this world, it happens to everyone, so do not feel desire and yearning for this life. Even if you feel desire and yearning you cannot stay, you can only wander in saṁsāra.'

The Tibetan Book of the Dead aptly describes the psychology of the dying man on hearing the prayers offered for his peaceful end:

> Now when the bardo of dharmatā dawns upon me, I will abandon all thoughts of fear and terror, I will recognise whatever appears as my projection and know it to be a vision of the bardo; now that I have reached this crucial point I will not fear the peaceful and wrathful

ones, my own projections.

For his life after death prayers and gifts are offered so that he may not have to suffer the dearth of anything, material or spiritual. Gifts are offered with rare generosity; the person performing the last rites is encouraged to loosen his purse strings and offer whatever gifts he can in cash or in kind, the gifts which are meant to enable the dead to be ferried from the world of karmic miseries to the world of Elysian bliss or to the abode of the blessed. A *locus classicus* in the *Garuḍa Purāṇa* lauds liberality in making gift-offerings:

> By offering gifts of wealth to brāhmaṇas, the sons in fact, prepare for their salvation along with sons, grandsons and great grandsons. What is given to father will be requited a hundredfold; to a mother a thousandfold; to a sister a hundred thousandfold and to a brother manyfold.

Written with ungrudging assistance given by Digvijay Narayan Singh, a scholar *par excellence*, the following pages deal with the rite of śrāddha and vindicate the popular belief that śrāddha, being an important topic, forms an integral part of Hindu dharmaśāstra. "The belief in the after-death survival of deceased ancestors and their separate world (pitṛ-loka)", observes a commentator, "belongs to the Indo-Iranian period and as such is pre-vedic . . . Ancestor-worship for one's prosperity, continuation of one's race is as old as the *Ṛg Veda*." It appears that the ritual of śrāddha prescribed by *Agni, Garuḍa, Kūrma, Padma, Viṣṇu Purāṇas* practically follows the same procedure as given in the *Gṛhyasūtras* and smṛtis of Manu and Yājñavalkya. "If the author of a Purāṇa follows a particular *sūtra"*, the commentator adds, "he prescribes the procedure of his *sūtra*. For example, in the present case, the procedure of śrāddha given in the *Nārada Purāṇa* shows much resemblance to the details given in the *Śrāddha*

Sūtra of Kātyāyana (which by the way has so much similarity with the procedure of śrāddha given in the *Yājñavalkya Smṛti*)."

Grateful thanks are due to Mr. J.P. Jain of Messrs. Motilal Banarsidass Publishers Private Limited, Delhi, for initiating this purposeful project which began with a description of the Hindu marriage system. This volume completes the series, ending as it does with a description of the last saṁskāra. As soon as the players have played their seven parts the eighth is played by the descendants, preferably by the son of the deceased. What begins with the garbhādhāna (now outlandish to many) comes full circle with the completion of the śrāddha.

The saṁskāras do not leave out any of the seven stages nor any of the turning points in the life of an orthodox Hindu. It is considered meritorious to remember the dead and pay the deceased ancestors due homage and obeisance.

Cordial thanks are also due to several pandits, purohitas, and priests who have preceded me and by their writings paved the way for this little volume.

R.C. Prasad

Introduction

Of the sixteen saṁskāras which encompass a Hindu life the last one is performed for the dead by their sons or grandsons or relatives. Many passages in the purāṇas and dharmaśāstras extoll the role of the son in the life of a devout Hindu; in that of a non-believer and heretic, a relative is as important as a son insofar as the last rites are concerned. Manu's views, widely known and held by those professing orthodox Hinduism, are quite explicit on this issue:

अकृता वा कृता वाऽपि यं विन्देत्सदृशात्सुतम् ।
पौत्री मातामहस्तेन दद्यात्पिण्डं हरेद्धनम् ॥
पुत्रेण लोकाञ्जयति पौत्रेणानन्त्यमश्नुते ।
अथ पुत्रस्य पौत्रेण ब्रध्नस्याप्नोति विष्टपम् ॥
पुन्नाम्नो नरकाद्यस्मात्त्रायते पितरं सुतः ।
तस्मात्पुत्र इति प्रोक्तः स्वयमेव स्वयंभुवा ॥

Manu Smṛti, IX-136-8

akṛtā vā kṛtā vā'pi yaṁ vindetsadṛśātsutam ।
pautrī mātāmahastena dadyātpiṇḍaṁ hareddhanam ॥
putreṇa lokāñjayati pautreṇānantyamaśnute ।
atha putrasya pautreṇa bradhnasyāpnoti viṣṭapam ॥
punnāmno narakādyasmāttrāyate pitaraṁ sutaḥ ।
tasmātputra iti proktaḥ svayameva svayaṁbhuvā ॥

"Through that son whom a daughter, either not appointed or appointed, may bear to a husband of equal caste, his maternal grandfather has a son's son; he shall present the funeral cake and take the estate. Through a son he conquers the worlds, through a son's son he obtains immortality, but through his son's grandson he gains the world of the sun. Because a son delivers (*trāyate*) his father from the hell called Put, he was therefore called put-tra (a deliverer from Put) by the Self-existent (Svayambhū) himself."

In the twenty-ninth chapter of the *Garuḍa Purāṇa* we are told, though in different words, that there is no salvation for a man without a son; he can never attain heaven without a son. The purāṇa goes a step further when it declares that one must obtain a son somehow. In the forty-third chapter 'On Performing a Śrāddha' of the *Garuḍa Purāṇa* a persona of the author, the Lord, is made to proclaim thus:

> Either the mother or a kinsman can perform the expiatory rite on behalf of a boy less than twelve but above four. Boys of less than four years in age can never be guilty or sinful. Even the king cannot punish them. There is no expiatory rite prescribed for such boys, in the śāstras.

That the śrāddha, if performed according to the dharmaśāstras, led to the everlasting peace of the departed soul and liberated it from karmic bonds and from the cycles of birth and death is widely recognized. This explains why so much attention is paid to this ritual by the ancient seers. Some of them give a detailed description of the funeral rites and of subsequent rituals at the crematorium or at home. In the *Nārada Purāṇa,* for example, one finds a description of the śrāddha rites as well as qualifications of the brāhmaṇa invitee to the rituals. Realizing the pre-eminence of the last rites among the saṁskāras, the law-givers also lay down some mandatory disqualifications of an invitee as well as rules with regard to the śrāddha-tithis.

According to the *Nārada Purāṇa,* only a brāhmaṇa who has some special merits can be invited for a śrāddha. He should be well-versed in the Vedas, devoted to Viṣṇu and abider by his own conventional conduct of life, and born of a good family and be of quiet nature. Among the characteristics of such a brāhmaṇa are also his dispassion and freedom from hatred. "He should be an expert in the interpretation of the purāṇas", says the *Nārada Purāṇa.* "He must be conversant with the *madhu* verses and must have studied the *tri-suparṇa.* He should be engaged in the worship of the deities and be an adept in the principles of smṛtis. He must be a pastmaster in the knowledge of the principles of the Upaniṣads. He must be interested in the welfare of all worlds. He should be grateful and richly endowed with all good qualities. He must be engaged in advising others by recounting the good scriptural texts. These are the brāhmaṇas who can be employed in a śrāddha."

As for the disqualifications of an invitee, the same (Nārada) purāṇa says:

> One who is physically deformed, wanting in a limb or by having a superfluous limb, a miser, a sickly person, a leper, one with deformed nails, a person with long suspended ears, one who has broken his religious vows, a person whose livelihood is the reading of the stars (i.e. astrology), he who professionally burns corpses, a person indulgent in heretical arguments, the younger brother who marries when the elder brother is yet a bachelor; a professional worshipper of idols, a rogue, a person who speaks ill of others; a hot-tempered person, a knave, the village priest, one who is interested in unholy scriptures, one who is devoted to and dependent on other men's food, one who supports the son of a śūdra woman, the paramour of a śūdra woman, kuṇḍas and golakas (i.e. bastards born of adultery when the husband is alive or when the husband is dead), one who performs yajña of those who are not eligible to perform it, a man of fraudulent conduct, a man who

shaves off his head without purpose, one who is enamoured of another man's wife or wealth, one who is devoid of devotion to Śiva, those who sell the Vedas (i.e. accept fee for recitation and teaching of the Vedas), the sellers of vratas, those who sell smṛtis and mantras, professional musicians, composers of poems, those who maintain themselves by means of practising medicine for money, one who is engaged in decrying the Vedas, arsonists of villages and forests, one who is over passionate, one who sells intoxicating beverages and one who indulges in deceitful arguments. All these should be excluded scrupulously from the śrāddha.

He should invite the brāhmaṇa the previous day or on the same day. The brāhmaṇa who is invited should maintain celibacy and conquer his sense organs.

As soon as a competent brāhmaṇa gifted with all the qualifications laid down here has been discovered and found willing to supervise and direct the śrāddha rituals, the householder, with his sense-organs duly subdued, should take the darbha grass in his hands and invite the intelligent brāhmaṇa with following words: "O excellent Sir, you should do me a favour and accept my invitation for śrāddha." On his part, the householder is required to get up early in the morning and perform the daily morning routine. The learned man should perform the śrāddha at the hour called Kutapa (i.e. the eighth muhūrta or five hours and thirty-six minutes after the sunrise). That hour in the eighth kāla (muhūrta) of the day when the sun begins to be less fierce is called the Kutapa. That which is given to the pitṛs at that time is of everlasting benefit. The afternoon is the time granted to the pitṛs by the self-born deity (god Brahmā). Hence, the kavya (oblations to the pitṛs) should be given by excellent brāhmaṇas only at that time. If the kavya is offered along with the monetary gifts at the wrong hour it should be known as belonging to the rākṣasas. It never reaches the pitṛs. The kavya offered in the evening too becomes something pertaining to the rākṣasas. The giver as well as the partaker of food falls into hell.

It should be borne in mind that the śrāddha rituals are but a form of ancestor worship, which is based on the belief in after-death survival of the deceased ancestors and their residence in a particular region called pitṛ-loka. It is an important topic and forms an integral part of Hindu dharmaśāstras. This belief is pre-vedic as it dates back to the Indo-Iranian period. Ancestor-worship was deemed essential for the continuation of one's race and prosperity to one's family.

There is an interesting dialogue between Śaṁśapāyana and Sūta in the *Vāyu Purāṇa* which has śrāddha for its theme. Śaṁśapāyana, inquisitive to his finger tips, thus questions the wise Sūta:

> What śrāddhas are to be offered to the pitṛs? How do these śrāddhas reach the pitṛs—the śrāddhas that are offered uttering the names of father, father's father and great-grandfather—against the rice-balls (piṇḍas)? How are they (pitṛs), if stationed in hell, competent to grant benefits? Who are these called by the name pitṛs? Whom shall we worship again? We have heard that even devas in heaven worship the pitṛs.

Unperturbed, Sūta said quietly:

> A śrāddha of the human beings is what is offered with faith. Brahmā created devas but they did not worship him. They forsook him and desirous of fruits for themselves created themselves. They were cursed by Brahmā—"O deluded ones! You will all become devoid of sense." They did not know anything. Then the whole world became deluded. All of them bowed to god Brahmā and implored him. In order to bless the worlds, the Lord spoke to them again. "Perform expiatory rites for the transgression which has been committed. As your

sons and therefrom you will attain knowledge." Desirous of knowing the procedure of expiatory rites, devas controlled themselves duly and asked their own sons mutually. Those sons who were conversant with real dharma and possessed self-control, explained to them the various modes of expiatory rites—verbal, mental and physical. The heaven-dwellers who regained their senses became delighted and spoke to their sons—"You are our fathers (pitṛs), since we are enlightened by you. What boon should be granted—virtue, knowledge or love?" Then Brahmā spoke to them—"You are the speakers of truth. Hence what is spoken by you shall be so and not otherwise. This is what is uttered by you—your sons have been mentioned by you as your pitṛs (fathers). They will be your pitṛs. Let this boon be given to them." On account of the words of Brahmā, Parameṣṭhin, the sons (pitṛs) attained the status of fathers of devas and devas, the real fathers, the status of sons. Hence it is declared in the dharmaśāstra that the sons of devas are pitṛs and the status of pitṛ-hood is proclaimed about them.

After declaring in this manner that the fathers are the sons and the sons are the pitṛs (fathers), God Brahmā addressed to them again for the development of their own selves. "If anyone will perform any holy rite without worshipping the pitṛs in a śrāddha, rākṣasas and dānavas will obtain the fruit thereof. The pitṛs propitiated and developed by means of śrāddha develop the imperishable Soma. Propitiated and developed by you all, they will always increase."

Sūta then goes on to describe the advantages accruing from the performance of śrāddha. In no case are the pitṛs satisfied unless propitiated by means of śrāddhas. When they are thus propitiated, they develop the imperishable Soma (the moon-god), who develops the people and the entire world, along with mountains and forests surrounded by mobile and immobile beings. Enlarging on the benefits resulting from the ritual of śrāddha performed in accordance with the rules laid down in the scriptures, Sūta says:

> Those men, who, desirous of nourishment, perform śrāddhas are always granted development and progeny of the pitṛs.Those pitṛs to whom they (the performers of śrāddha) offer three balls of rice mentioning their names and gotra up to great-grandfather, they (pitṛs) who are present everywhere, strengthen and develop their progeny by that offering of śrāddha. Such a behest has been declared formerly by the supreme god Brahmā. It is by their grace that dāna (charitable gift), adhyayana (Vedic study) and tapas (penance) fructify. There is no doubt in this that pitṛs grant you perfect knowledge. In this manner pitṛs are devas and devas are pitṛs. Devas and pitṛs are reciprocally pitṛs.

The *Vāyu Purāṇa*, a veritable repertoire of instructions for the śrāddha-offerers, answers a number of questions put by the sages to Sūta. These mainly relate to the pitṛs. When the sages asked:

> What is the reason for which the pitṛs are worshipped at the outset in every yajña? All the holy rites of noble souls begin with the performance of śrāddhas. To whom all these śrāddhas are to be offered? What is the great benefit when they are offered? In which of the holy centres and sacred rivers does the śrāddha performance yield ever-lasting benefit? What are those holy centres in which excellent brāhmaṇas ought to perform śrāddha to obtain all desired benefits? What is the proper time for śrāddha? What is the procedure to be followed?

Bṛhaspati informs them that śrāddha offered to the pitṛs never goes in vain. The manes, duly propitiated in (sic) śrāddha, nourish Soma (the moon) making use of their yogic power whereby the three worlds maintain their lives. "Hence", adds Bṛhaspati, "śrāddhas must always be offered to yogins with special efforts. Indeed, the mainstay of the pitṛs is yoga and from (thanks to) yoga the moon functions." That in all antyeṣṭi rites the homage paid to the pitṛs occupies an eminently important position, cannot be questioned. The following table of the pitṛs would give a fair idea of their status and class:

Class of the pitṛs	*Names of their daughter and other particulars*
Vairājas	Menā, wife of Himavān, mother of Umā, Śiva's consort.
Barhiṣads	Acchodā, adopted king Amāvasu as father; cursed by pitṛs; became Satyavatī, mother of Vyāsa and queen of Śāntanu.
Agniṣvāttas	Pīvarī, married to Śuka, Vyāsa's son.
Kāvyas (sons of Agni and Svadhā)	Yogotpatti alias Ekaśṛṅgā married Śuka.
Upahūtas (sons of Aṅgiras)	Yaśodā, queen mother of King Khaṭvāṅga.
Ājyapas (sons of Pulaha)	Virajā, married to King Nahuṣa, mother of Yayāti.
Sukāla (sons of Vasiṣṭha)	Narmadā (the river), wife of Purukutsa and mother of Trasad-dasyu.

It is widely held that intellect, nourishment, power of memory, brain, kingdom and health can be attained only through the grace of the noble-souled pitṛs. The *Vāyu Purāṇa* is of the view that:

> Pitāmahas grant crores of gems, pearls, *lapis lazuli*, garments and thousands of horses and elephants. Pitāmahas always bestow on men chariots fitted with

swans and peacocks, studded with pearls and *lapis lazuli* and decorated with tinkling bells and provided with perpetual flowers and fruits.

Bṛhaspati, realizing what the śrāddha rites are meant for the manes, lays stress on the solemnity with which they should be performed. The vessels meant for the pitṛs should be made of gold, silver or copper. A silver or silver-coated vessel is said to be acceptable to the pitṛs. What Bṛhaspati says relates to pitṛ-śrāddhas and not to obsequial rites performed at the death of a kinsman. If the former (pitṛ-śrāddha) is the goal, showing or gifting away of silver is a suitable gift for the pitṛs and it is conducive to the attainment of infinite and everlasting heaven. Good sons enable the pitṛs to cross hell by means of this religious gift. The reason why the silver vessel is highly spoken of is that svadhā was formerly milked by the pitṛs seeking to get svadhā. If the destruction of demons is desired—and desired it shall be—then the nearby presence, sight or gifting away of the hide of a black antelope should be recommended. It increases brāhmaṇical splendour and enables the pitṛs to cross hell.

Bṛhaspati singles out certain objects as holy. They are: vessels made of gold, silver or copper, gingelly seeds, garments, *tridaṇḍi-yoga* (i.e. the yoga of mind, speech and body), Kutapa (i.e. the eighth muhūrta of the day), kuśa grass and sesamum seeds—all sacred enough for use in most of the Hindu saṁskāras. The actual procedure to be followed in performing the śrāddha rituals as given by Bṛhaspati in the *Vāyu Purāṇa* is as follows:

> In the south-east direction, especially at the intermediate point corner between them, should be the place for śrāddha. It should be well-situated and square shaped with sides equal to an aratni (the distance between the tip of the fist and the elbow).

Bṛhaspati mentions the proper spot for the holy rites

of the pitṛs in accordance with the injunctions of the scriptures. It is conducive to the attainment of wealth, health and longevity. It enhances strength and brightness of complexion. At the place intended for srāddha, three pits should be dug and three sticks of khadira wood should be placed. They (the sticks) should be an aratni in length and should be embellished with silver bands. The pits should be a vitasti (the span or the distance between thumb and little finger when they are extended on either side) in depth and the four sides should be four aṅgulas (fingers) each.

The sticks should not be hollow and they must be placed on the ground with their faces pointing to the south-east. The performer of śrāddha should be pure and should wash them with holy waters or water rendered holy by the use of the ring of darbha grass called pavitra worn by the performer of śrāddha. The purification (śodhana) may be carried out with goat's milk or cow's milk and water. By means of this tarpaṇa (holy water-offering) the satisfaction of the pitṛs will be permanent. He will be prosperous here and hereafter. He will be blessed with the fruits of all holy rites. If a person always takes bath three times a day and worships the pitṛs with the prescribed mantras, he gets the fruit of performance of a horse-sacrifice (Aśvamedha).

On the new moon day, the śrāddha materials should be placed in the pit in the ground four aṅgulas square. These rituals are called *triḥ-sapta-yajña* (three-times seven yajña). All the three worlds are sustained by them. He will attain nourishment, prosperity, longevity and progeny. Various types of fortune will resort to him and he will gradually attain liberation from saṁsāra. It removes sins. It sanctifies. It has the same fruit as a horse-sacrifice. The mantra has been composed by Brahmā. It is the amṛta (immortal or nectarine) and it is honoured and worshipped by brāhmaṇas and grants the fruit of Aśvamedha.

The Mantra: "Obeisance to all the deities, to the pitṛs, to the great yogins, to svadhā. Obeisance forever to svāhā." At the beginning and the conclusion of the śrāddha, this mantra shall always be repeated three times. The devotee shall repeat this with purity of mind, when he offers the balls of rice also. The pitṛs arrive quickly and demons flee. Regularly repeated at the time of śrāddha by the expounders of Brahman, this mantra enables the pitṛs to cross hell in the three worlds. A person desirous of kingdom, should always repeat this mantra with alertness. It increases virility, purity, wealth, sāttvika qualities, prosperity, longevity and strength.

The Saptārcis Mantra, said to be extremely auspicious, bestows all desires. By repeating it regularly, the pitṛs are propitiated. The mantra rendered into English, is this: "I always make obeisance to those who are engaged in meditation by means of the yogic vision, to the embodied and unembodied pitṛs of brilliant splendour. I bow to the Seven Sages and the pitṛs who fulfil all desires and who are the progenitors of Indra and other devas and of Bhṛgu and Mārīca (Kaśyapa).

"After bowing to all the pitṛs who bestow welfare on Manu and other lords of suras and on the sun and the moon, I bow down with palms joined in reverence to pitāmahas, the progenitors of the constellations, the mobile and the immobile beings and of the heaven and the earth. With palms joined in reverence I bow down to those who bestow fearlessness, to those who are revered by all the worlds and to the progenitors of the divine sages. With palms joined in reverence, I bow down to Prajāpati, Kaśyapa, Soma, Varuṇa and to the lords of all yoga.

"Obeisance to the seven groups of the pitṛs in the seven worlds. Obeisance to the self-born Brahmā of yogic vision".

Thus the mantra honoured by the groups of Brahmarṣis

along with the Seven Sages has been mentioned. It is highly holy and sanctified. It is conducive to prosperity and destructive of rākṣasas. The man who performs śrāddha according to these injunctions attains three boons. The pitṛs grant food, longevity and children to the people on the earth. He who is endowed with great devotion, who has faith, who has controlled his senses and who always repeats this Saptārcis Mantra with purity, becomes the sole Emperor on the earth consisting of seven continents and oceans.

If anything is cooked in the house, whether a dainty or ordinary eatable, it should never be eaten in that house without first offering it to deities. Henceforth, I shall describe in the proper order, the vessels intended for oblations to the pitṛs. Even as I mention listen to the respective benefits in using oblations in the different vessels.

The scriptures declare that a leaf of the palāśa tree (*Butea frondosa*) is conducive to brāhmaṇic splendour. That kingdom is conceived as the fruit, if leaves of the aśvattha tree are used. The Lordship of all living beings is mentioned in using the leaves of plakṣa (citron-leaved Indian fig tree) [i.e. the materials of oblations must be placed in cups made of these leaves or the wood as in the case of some of the following].

Those who are desirous of prosperity, wisdom, intellect and power of memory shall use the leaves of the banyan tree. The vessel of the leaves of kāśmarī (a large tree called gambhārī also) is conducive to fame and destructive of demons. That which is offered in the madhūka tree (*Bassia latifolia*) is considered excellent and conducive to good fortune. One who performs śrāddha in the vessel of phalgu (a kind of fig tree) attains all desires.

The performer attains supreme lustre, particularly all-round brilliance if the sun-plant is used. By using a bilva vessel, riches, intellect and longevity are always attained.

If śrāddha is performed in bamboo vessels, Parjanya (cloud or the lord of rain) always showers in his fields, parks, lakes and all crops. It is said in the śāstras that those who make śrāddha offerings even for once in these excellent vessels, attain the fruit of all yajñas. He who always offers fragrant garlands to the pitṛs becomes endowed with riches and glory, and shines brilliantly like the sun. He who offers incense, fragrant gum-resin and other things to the pitṛs, along with honey and ghī obtains the fruit of a horse-sacrifice. He who offers shining fragrant dhūpa, incense to the pitṛs begets children beneficial to him here and hereafter. Hence he shall always offer it to the pitṛs.

He who always offers lamp to the pitṛs assiduously, obtains unequalled auspicious power of vision in the world. He becomes brilliant on the earth. He shines in heaven with splendour, fame, refulgence and strength. He rejoices in the aerial chariot surrounded by apsarās. He should offer scents, flowers, incense and ghī. After propitiating the pitṛs at the outset with fruits, roots and obeisance, with purity of mind and body, the devotee should later worship brāhmaṇas with food and wealth. Always at the time of śrāddha, pitāmahas (manes) assume aerial forms and on seeing brāhmaṇas, they enter them. Hence the excellent brāhmaṇas should be honoured with garments, foodstuffs, charitable gifts, food and beverages, gifts of cows, horses and villages. If brāhmaṇas are honoured, the pitṛs become delighted. One should, therefore, honour excellent brāhmaṇas duly.

In the holy rite of śrāddha, brāhmaṇas should perform diligently the ritualistic scraping, digging and sprinkling of water with darbha ullekhana and prokṣaṇa by means of the left and the right hands. A learned man should keep ready for libation darbhas, balls of rice, foodstuffs, different kinds of flowers, scents, charitable gifts and ornaments. After propitiating the persons present duly, the brāhmaṇas shall perform the Vaiśvadeva rite and then perform the rites with abhyaṅga (oil bath) with darbha (leaves of the kuśa grass) in accordance with the injunctions. The excellent food-offering to the pitṛs should be made with reverse wearing of the sacred thread. After pronouncing the names of pitṛs the thread must be offered to all of them in lieu of garments. The rites of khaṇḍana, prokṣaṇa and ullekhana are to be performed only once in the case of devas, and thrice in the case of pitṛs. Wearing a single pavitra (a ringlike loop of kuśa grass worn round a finger) in the hand and reciting the Cailamantra, the balls of rice are touched once for each of the pitṛs. Then the benefit of showing is attained.

Always the balls of rice must be offered on the ground along with ghī and gingelly seeds. The devotee performing pitṛ-śrāddha, kneels on the ground with the left knee touching it. He invokes the fathers, grandfathers and great-grandfathers and all ancestry of yore and properly sprinkles all round the balls of rice, by means of the holy water (pitṛtīrtha) carefully from the right to the left in anticlockwise manner. Some men desire a separate śrāddha for maternal grandfathers by means of food, water, flowers and foodstuffs of various kinds. He should offer three *piṇḍas* in the proper order pressing them with the thumb. They are conducive to the enhancement of nourishment. He should offer the *piṇḍas* by means of both hands placed between the knees. In offering the *piṇḍas* the left hand should be placed over the right, repeating the mantra '*Namo vaḥ pitaraḥ saumyāḥ*' always carefully in this manner.

Carefully repeating the mantra '*Namo vaḥ pitaraḥ saumyāḥ*' (Obeisance to ye, O gentle pitṛs) he should offer the first *piṇḍa* with both the hands and place it in the southern quarter.

With both the hands, he draws the outline of a mortar using the water from the water pot. He must be careful in the practice of piety. He should offer a fresh thread of silk or jute or a cotton thread. Woven silk, such coloured cloth and kauśeya should be avoided when offering thread to the pitṛs. In the sacrifice, the thread taken even from a freshly woven cloth shall be avoided. These do not please the pitṛs. Those who give these cannot flourish.

The collyrium obtained from the Trikūṭa mountain, they say, is always excellent. So also is the oil extracted from black gingelly seeds. Sandal, agaru (fragrant aloe wood), tamāla, uśīra (fragrant root of the plant *Andropogon Muricatus),* lotus, fragrant incense, gum resin and white turuṣka—all these are excellent articles for use in śrāddha. White flowers are excellent. So also the red and blue lotuses. All other flowers can be used if they are fragrant. The flowers china rose, bhāṇḍīra, upakāma and kuraṇḍaka should always be avoided in the śrāddha rite. Odourless flowers and flowers of obnoxious odour should be avoided at that time by one who seeks prosperity.

The brāhmaṇas invited on that occasion should invariably face the north while sitting. The performer of the śrāddha should duly face the south. He should face them and offer the darbhas and the *piṇḍas.* He should worship his own grandfathers by means of this rite.

The following objects are said to be essential in a śrāddha: Green piñjalīs (leaves of kuśa grass) as smooth and soft as flowers, about aratni in size, softened and straightened by the holy water (pitṛtīrtha), blue near the root and not defiled by pebbles etc. should be used. So also śyāmāka and nīvāra kinds of rice. This story has been narrated by the excellent Prajāpati. His hairs fell down through the path of the sky on the earth. Hence the kāśa grasses are holy. They are always honoured in the śrāddha rite. The piṇḍas are to be offered on them by one who wishes prosperity. Those who do so become free from sins and defects. Their children become nourished with splendour, fame and refulgence.

The devotee should sit facing the south and spread the darbha grass once for the piṇḍas. The tips of the darbhas should be pointing to the south-east. The procedure shall be mentioned as follows: A learned man should always perform śrāddha with concentration of mind. He shall neither be dejected nor angry. His mind should not be distracted or diverted elsewhere.

The following mantra is to be repeated: "I annihilate everything that has impurity in it. All asuras and dānavas have been killed by me. All rākṣasas, yakṣas, groups of piśācas and all yātudhānas (demons) have been killed by me." All asuras avoid him who offers food to the pitṛs by repeating this mantra. Rākṣasas avoid the place where this mantra is recited. A brāhmaṇa should always perform śrāddha according to this procedure. The manes (pitāmahas) will grant whatever is desired in the mind by him.

If śrāddha is always performed assiduously, the pitṛs become delighted in mind and rākṣasas become dejected. Śūdras should always avoid the following in śrāddha: *kṣīraniryāsa* (trees yielding white juice), trees called balvaja (*Eluesine Indica*, a species of coarse grass not liked by cattle) and other kinds of grasses such as vāraṇa, lava, lava-varṣa. They shall avoid applying collyrium, oil and unguents as well as wearing garlands. Their rites should be performed with kāśas which grow again when cut. All the benefits accrue to them thereby. Kāśa grass and the regrown kāśa grass are like peacock's tail and its regrowth. So the pitṛs are devas and devas are pitṛs. This is the mantra intended for flowers, incense, scents etc. Pulling the vessel of materials of worship towards the south assiduously for the sake of homa, he (performer of śrāddha) should repeat the mantra: "Svadhā unto Soma, the pitṛmān (having pitṛs). Obeisance to Aṅgiras." He should perform the homa of non-heavenly or the worldly type for the purpose of the fructification of the holy rite.

Homa is to be performed after placing samit (sacrificial twig) within. The devotee should keep the mind perfectly pure and keep the holy fire scrupulously pure, repeating the mantra: "Svadhā unto Agni, the bearer of kavya. Obeisance to Aṅgiras. Svadhā and obeisance unto Yama and Aṅgiras." These are the mantras in order intended for homas. Homas shall be performed everyday from the southern direction to Agni and to Soma in the middle. In between these two homas, a homa should be performed to Vivasvān (the Sun or his son Yama). *Upacāras* (ways of rendering homage), repetition of svadhā mantra, ullekhana (ritualistic scrubbing), homas, japas, obeisance, particularly prokṣaṇa (sprinkling), applying collyrium, oil bath and offering piṇḍas—all these must be performed. If they are performed with mantras, they have the same benefit as a horse-sacrifice. All holy rites mentioned above shall be assiduously performed.

In the blazing fire plenty of ghī must be offered. Particularly homa must be performed in a smokeless fire with curly leaping flames, for the fructification of the holy rite. We have heard that if a yajamāna performs homa in a weakly burning smoking fire, he becomes blind and issueless. If there is deficiency of fuel, if the flames are defiled by smoke, the fire is not conducive to good results. If the fire emits bad odour, if the flames are bluish or particularly black, or if the fire makes the ground crack, know that there is failure in the holy rite. The resplendent fire with a single globular flame, yellowish (golden) in colour, produced by the ghī, is conducive to the fructification of the rite. The flame shall be smooth and curling clockwise. That fire is perpetually honoured and worshipped by both men and women. Thereby, the everlasting pitṛs become honoured and worshipped. They give everlasting benefits.

Mud-pots, vessels made of the leaves or wood of the udumbara (*Ficus Glomerata*) tree, its fruits and samits, all these are considered very holy in śrāddha. They are very pure. The different benefits of the various kinds of vessels that I have mentioned as regards the śrāddha rite, O excellent brāhmaṇas, are also true in regard to the holy rites of nativity. With regard to the samits also, the same should be known. The devotee keeps the mind pure and says, 'I am performing the rite in fire'. Then, after being permitted by excellent brāhmaṇas, saying 'Do', he should perform the homa in the fire, accompanied by his wife and sons. The following trees are equally sacrifice-worthy: palāśa, plakṣa, nyagrodha, aśvattha, vikaṅkaṭa, bilva and candana.

The following trees are particularly recommended for the purpose of samits (sacrificial twigs): sarala, devadāru, śāla and khadira. Rural thorny trees are also sacrifice-worthy. Some of them are honoured for the purpose of samits in accordance with the words of the pitṛs. Even as I recount, listen to the fruit of the holy rite to those who perform homa with the samits of the Kalkaphala (pomegranate) tree. The aloe wood is to be desired by all. It has the same benefit as that of a horse-sacrifice. The following trees should be avoided—śleṣmātaka, naktamāla, kapittha, śālmali, nīpa, vibhītaka and the creepers also. Similarly the trees on which birds reside must be avoided. Those trees which are considered unworthy of sacrifice should also be avoided. In the course of the sacrificial rite, the word svadhā is used at the end of the mantra pertaining to the pitṛs and svāhā is used in the case of devas.

Sūta said: Bṛhaspati declared in reply that as per injunctions of the *Atharva Veda*, devas are the pitṛs but there are also other pitṛs. One should especially worship the pitṛs before devas. People in the world do worship the pitṛs before devas.

Dakṣa had a daughter famous in the world by the name of Viśvā. O knower of dharma, she was given duly and righteously to Dharma. It is well-known that her sons are the noble-souled Viśvedevas. They were very famous throughout the three worlds. They were revered by all the people in the world. On the beautiful peak of Himavān resorted to by devas and gandharvas, all those noble souls performed a very severe penance, performed by all the apsarās and resorted to by all the devas and gandharvas.

The delighted pitṛs spoke to them with a pure (frank) mind—"We are delighted. Request for a boon. What desire of yours shall we fulfil?" When this was mentioned by the pitṛs, Brahmā, the creator of the three worlds, the Lord of the subjects, spoke to the Viśvas (Viśvedevas).

Brahmā said: "Even Mahādeva of great brilliance, has been scorched by them by means of the great penance. I am well-delighted by that penance. What desire of yours shall I fulfil?" Thus urged by Brahmā, the creator of the world, all of them simultaneously spoke to Brahmā, the creator of the world, "May we have a share in śrāddha. This is the boon desired by us." Then Brahmā spoke to them who were worshipped in the heaven "What you desire will take place." The pitṛs said, "So be it", and continued, "There is no doubt about it. Whatever is performed here shall be for you too along with us. In the śrāddha intended by men for us, you will get the priority in being seated. We are telling you the truth. They will worship you at the outset by means of garlands, scents and food offerings.

Everything will be offered to you first and then to us. Our ritualistic farewell will occur first and the devatās (i.e. you) will be ritualistically dismissed later. The protection of śrāddha and (according) of hospitality—these are the two ceremonial acts to be performed in the rite of śrāddha offered to the pitṛs and devatās and bhūtas. If it is done duly according to injunctions, everything shall be all right."

After granting them the boon thus, Lord Brahmā, the benefactor of all living beings, went away happily along with the groups of the pitṛs. Five great yajñas have been prescribed in the Vedas. A man shall always perform these five mahāyajñas. Listen to and understand where the performers of those five yajñas go and where their abode is. They attain the abode of Brahman that is fearless, devoid of egotism, free from sorrow, strainless and free from pain. It yields all desires. These five yajñas are to be performed by a śūdra also, but without reciting the mantras. He who eats (enjoys) otherwise without performing them, eats debts everyday. He who cooks for himself is a sinful soul and he eats debts. Hence a sensible man shall perform the five great yajñas. Some wish that naivedya (food-offering) should be assiduously offered along with libation of water. The water-pot also shall be offered. The oblation should be made well announced. It shall be scattered by throwing it far above. Small oblations shall at first be offered on the horns of cows.

The piṇḍa cannot be offered as "naivedya" to the pitṛs. They should be duly fed by offering palatable foods and edibles. I am emphatically mentioning this as the procedure laid down in the Vedas. These groups of pitṛs are noble souls and lords of devas. Some preceptors wish that brāhmaṇas should be worshipped first everyday, and then the piṇḍa should be offered. But Bṛhaspati says to those who are experts in matters of dharma, practice of rituals, that he (the performer of śrāddha) should offer the piṇḍa first and feed the brāhmaṇas later. For the pitṛs are born of yoga, yogic power and are themselves yogic souls and great ones. The pitṛs strengthen and develop Soma (the Moon). Hence he (the performer of śrāddha), remaining pure and devotedly attached to yogins, should offer the piṇḍas to yogins. This shall be the havis offering directly to the pitṛs.

If a single yogin be in the seat of priority among thousands of brāhmaṇas, he will enable the yajamāna and the brāhmaṇas partaking of the food, cross the ocean of worldly existence like a boat in water. Where the wicked are accepted and honoured and where the good are disrespected, a terrible punishment meted out by the devas befalls them immediately. If a pious brāhmaṇa who has come as a guest is left out and a foolish one is fed, the householder forgoes his prior holy rites and perishes (i.e. despite his merit in a previous birth he is faced with ruin).

He who seeks enjoyment of worldly pleasures should assiduously consign the piṇḍa to the sacred fire. He who seeks progeny shall give the middle piṇḍa to his wife but after performing all the intervening rites and mantras. He who wishes for excellent refulgence always offers the piṇḍa to cows. So also he who wishes for intellect, honour, fame and renown, offers it always to cows. He who seeks long life gives it to crows. One desirous of comeliness offers oblations to the fowl. Thus the benefit of offering piṇḍas has been recounted. Or the devotee shall stand facing the south and to pacify the sky scatter the oblation in the sky. The abode of the pitṛs is the sky and their quarter is the south.

Further, brāhmaṇas mention one procedure of filling up the piṇḍa. After being permitted by brāhmaṇas who say, "Let it be taken up dry", the upper layer or the tip of flowers, fruits, edibles and cooked food shall be taken up and offered as oblation in the sacred fire. After consigning the edibles, cooked food, beverage and the excellent fruits to the fire, he should face the south and offer the piṇḍas. He shall propitiate them with oily edibles, sweet scents and juices. With concentration and purity of mind, he should serve them standing there with palms joined in reverence. A man devoted to them and full of faith, obtains the desires.

The grandfathers (manes) bestow the following qualities on him: the state of not being mean and low (non-pettiness), gratefulness, chivalry, hospitality and the ability for performance of sacrifices and religious gifts. Henceforth I shall recount the Saumya belonging to Soma procedure after the brāhmaṇas have taken food, in order. Listen to it, even as I recount it. The devotee attached to the pitṛs should sprinkle the ground and scrub it at the outset. Then he should scatter auspicious materials in accordance with the injunctions. He shall request the excellent brāhmaṇas to chant the svadhā mantra and offer them plenty of dakṣiṇās. He shall get the permission from them as to what should be done with the remnants of the food. With palms joined in reverence, he shall follow them after honouring them duly. He should then bid farewell.

Bṛhaspati said: Henceforth, I shall recount the various types of dānas (religious gifts) and the benefits thereof. I shall also mention the pure things to be used in the śrāddha rite and those that should be avoided. It should be performed on snow-capped precipice or he should also bring snow from there. Hence agnihotra is laid down in the scriptures as the greatest and the holiest. One shall avoid śrāddha-performance during the night. On other occasions also, since Rāhu is seen, one should quickly perform śrāddha as soon as Rāhu is seen even by spending one's entire possession. He who does not perform śrāddha at the time of eclipse becomes distressed like the cow stuck up in mire. He who performs it, uplifts sinners like a boat in the ocean that saves those who are drowning.

Formerly while Tvaṣṭṛ was being prevented by the noble-souled Lord of devas from drinking the soma juice meant for Indra, the consort of Śacī, it (some part or drops of soma) fell on the ground. *Śyāmākas* (a variety of rice) grew up that way from drops of soma. They are honoured for the propitiation of the pitṛs. The spray of soma juice sticking to and coming out of his nostrils fell from them and became *ikṣu*—sugarcane. Hence sugarcanes are phlegmatic, cool, pleasing and sweet. One should perform all the pitṛ-rites with śyāmāka rice and sugarcane for the fulfilment of all desires.

He who performs Āgrayaṇa, i.e. the first soma libation at the Agniṣṭoma sacrifice or of fruits after the rainy season with śyāmāka and sugarcanes attains the fulfilment of his desires quickly. Śyāmāka (rice), hastināman, paṭola (fruit of *Trichosanthes Diaoeca*), fruits of bṛhatī (brinjals) and the crest of Agastya—all are very astringent. Such other excellent and sweet things as nāgara, dīrghamūlaka (a kind of radish) should be offered at śrāddha. So also tender shoots of a bamboo, *surasa, sarjaka* (juicy parts of the sāla tree) and bhūstṛṇa (*Andropogen Schoenanthus*).

I shall now mention those things that should always be avoided in śrāddha. Garlic, carrots, onions, globular radish and *karambha* (groats or flour mixed with curds) and other articles devoid of smell and with no taste should be avoided in śrāddha. The reason is also mentioned as follows:

Formerly in the fight between devas and asuras, Bali was defeated by suras. From his wounds drops of blood gushed out and from them these articles grew up. Hence they are avoided in the śrāddha rite. The exudations mentioned in the Vedas, the salts found in arid lands are to be avoided in the śrāddha rites. Women in their monthly course shall not take part in śrāddhas.

Foul-smelling water, water having froth and foams, water from puddles, water where cows are disinclined to drink and the water stored in vessels the previous night shall not be used in śrāddha. The milk of ewes, deer, camel, single-horned animals, buffalo and the Camarī deer should be avoided by a wise man. Henceforth I shall mention the places that should be avoided assiduously. I shall also mention, by whom śrāddha should not be seen. I shall also recount what is pure and impure in a śrāddha. With great faith one should perform a śrāddha by means of fruits, roots and foodstuffs available in forests. Thereby he attains desirable country, heaven and liberation from saṁsāra as well as fame. Places full of noise-pollution and teeming with insects and a place with foul smell shall be avoided for the performance of śrāddha.

A place within a distance of twelve yojanas from all the rivers joining the sea (i.e. so far from their confluence with the sea), a door at the south-east as well as the land of Triśaṅku, should be avoided. The land to the north of Mahānadī and to the south of Kaikaṭa is the land of Triśaṅku. It is forbidden for the rite of śrāddha. The lands of Kāraṅkara (Karkal in south Kanara District), Kaliṅga, the land to the north of Sindhu and those lands wherein the practice of the pious rites of different stages of life and castes are not in vogue, should be avoided scrupulously. The naked and similar (apostates and non-Vedic sects) people should not see the śrāddha rite. This is the rule. Such śrāddhas as are seen by these, do not reach the pitṛs or pitāmahas.

Śaṁyu said: O holy Lord, O leader of important brāhmaṇas, please recount in detail and precisely to me who ask about the naked and similar people. Thus requested, Bṛhaspati of great brilliance said to him: The *Trayī* (the three Vedas) is remembered as the protective covering unto all living beings. Those who discard it out of delusion are the naked. If a man forsakes that protection, he becomes supportless and is ruined. If a man discards dharma and seeks liberation (*mokṣa*) elsewhere, his labour therein is in vain. For he has not the correct perspective.

Formerly, all the brāhmaṇas, kṣatriyas, vaiśyas and śūdras were made heretics and placed in a deformed state by asuras who were defeated in the battle between devas and asuras. This is not the creation of the self-born god Brahmā. Nor are these: Those who do not practise piety come under the category of "the naked and similar people" (nagnādayaḥ). A brāhmaṇa who keeps matted hair without any specific aim, who shaves off his hair for nothing and who goes about naked purposelessly is also called so. He who observes holy rites in vain, he who performs japas in vain is also called 'Naked etc.' So also those who blow off their homes, the hunters and those who destroy property are considered so. They are denounced as men of evil ways finding fault with every action committed. The śrāddha performed or witnessed by these, goes to men and not to the pitṛs.

The brāhmaṇa-slayer, the ungrateful, the atheists, the defilers of the preceptor's bed, robbers and wicked men are shunned at the very sight. One shall avoid all those who commit sins and particularly those who indulge in slandering devas and the divine sages. Whatever is witnessed by these, goes over to asuras and yātudhānas. Kṛtayuga is said to be the age of brāhmaṇas. Tretāyuga is remembered as the age of kṣatriyas. They say that Dvāparayuga is the age of vaiśyas and Kaliyuga is remembered as the age of śūdras.

The pitṛs said: The Vedas are to be worshipped in Kṛtayuga. Similarly suras are to be worshipped in Tretāyuga. Wars are always to be worshipped in Dvāpara and the heretics in Kaliyuga. There is no doubt in this that these spoil a śrāddha by their mere sight: the dishonoured, the unholy, fowl, domestic pig and dog. The śrāddha materials touched by calves and the people having pollution and chronic ailments are defiled. Cooked food should never be seen by dirty or fallen persons. If they see it, it cannot be used as havya and kavya (offerings to the gods and pitṛs). The chief materials touched by them become desecrated. Solidified ghī shall be avoided at the very outset. Sprinkling with water mixed with clay is laid down for the consecration of materials of śrāddha.

Scattering of yellow mustard and black gingelly seeds should be done. The articles should be assiduously shown to the preceptor, the sun and the fire. The following should be avoided in a śrāddha: that which is trodden upon by people while climbing on to their seats; that which is seen by the mobile beings that are defiled; dried up and stale things; partly eaten things, defiled objects; that which is licked at the tip; that which is defiled by gravel, pebbles and hair or worm-eaten; cooked rice and other foodstuffs in which salt has been added; gingelly seeds and barley ground and powdered like oilcake; and things shaken off from garments. There are certain people who profess to be very wise by showing their opposition to the Vedas. They are to be termed 'ayajñapatis' (non-masters of sacrifice). They are thought as the dusts of śrāddha. Forbidden vegetables mixed with curds, as well as sour gruel or fomented liquids are avoided in a śrāddha. One should avoid the egg-plant and all distilled liquors. The salt extracted from the ocean water and from the waters of the Mānasa lake is holy. This is extremely holy. It is visible directly. It is put into the fire and then taken in the hands and carefully pressed. It is to be applied to the forehead. This is remembered as Brahmatīrtha. All the articles for śrāddha should be sprinkled and offered in the sacrifice.

Ariṣṭa (soap-berry), tumula, bilva, iṅguda and śvasana should be soaked in water and water be sprinkled out of them. All sorts of baskets (wicker-work) should be purified according to the conventional practice. Vessels made of tooth (ivory)-bone, wood and horns should be scrubbed and scraped. All earthen pots should be burnt again for purification. Gems, diamonds, corals, pearls and conchs are to be purified by brushing with the residues of powdered yellow mustard or gingelly seeds. The same can be used to purify sheep wool and all types of hair.

All kinds of sheep's wool can be purified with clay and water, but at the beginning and end of all purificatory processes washing with water is recommended. Purification of cotton cloth is effected with sacred ashes. Flowers, fruits, pins and rods should be dipped in water. Purification of the earth (ground) is done by sweeping, sprinkling and smearing with cowdung. Outside the village the ground (earth) is purified by the wind. Purification (cleansing) of bow and arrows is effected by brushing them with clay. Thus the excellent modes of purification have been mentioned. Henceforth the pitṛs mention further modes of purification. One should evacuate the bowels early in the morning at a distance of an arrow-shot from the house in the south-western direction and within the view of the house. He should cover the head with a cloth. He shall not touch the head with the hands. Before evacuating the ground should be covered with dry grass, wooden sticks or leaves, bamboo chips or broken mud pots. He should take water in a pot and hold clay also in the hand in complete silence. He should sit facing the north during the day and the south during the night, wash his body thoroughly ensuring that his hands are also washed very clean before commencing the śrāddha.

Washing the feet after applying clay, he should duly perform ācamana (sipping of water). He should then pour water down three times with invocation of the sun, fire and water. A sensible man should always keep a water-pot handy. Subsidiary actions and washing of the feet shall be done by means of this pot. The performance of ācamana and divine duties shall be done by means of a second vessel. If such actions are performed with a defiled hand, one should observe fast for three nights. In protracted cases of default, the rite of Kṛcchra is prescribed for expiation. After touching a dog or a cāṇḍāla one should perform Taptakṛcchra rite.

If human bones are touched, fasting is the purification for it. It is prescribed that if the bones are touched deliberately, the fast is to be observed for three nights, and for one night, if touched unintentionally. By going to unholy places, one acquires all sorts of sins. These unholy places are—Kāraskaras, Pulindas, Āndhras, Śabaras and others, the land of Bhūtilaya if one drinks water there, the land of Yugandhara, up to the northern borderlands of Sindhu, the land of Divyantaraśata, sinful countries occupied by sinners and lands devoid of good men such as brāhmaṇas who have mastered the Vedas. Clarity of mind, fire, timely white-washing—these things indicate purity. But one is always ignorant. If one makes default in the purificatory rites—except out of ignorance, undoubtedly the benefit goes to piśācas and yātudhānas.

One who has no faith in purificatory rites is born among mlecchas. Those who do not perform yajñas and sinners are born among the lower strata of animals. A man gets released from sins through purificatory rites and attains heaven. Devas indeed desire purity. This has been declared by devas themselves. Suras always forsake the hideous and the unclean. Men of auspicious rites perform three types of purificatory rites justifiably. *Pitṛs* delighted with them for their pure rites, increase the yogic power and bestow all cherished things available in the three worlds, on these people, viz. a man who reveres brāhmaṇas, one who receives guests, an intelligent man who adheres to purity, one devotedly attached to parents, one who possesses self-control and one who is sympathetic.

Other purāṇas are not oblivious of the importance of the pitṛ-śrāddha.* What they are oblivious of is that though related to funeral rites—the subject of this volume—the śrāddha offered to the manes, is in certain details different. A perusal of this volume where the obsequial rites are described and of the different purāṇas where the annual ceremony of a śrāddha is dealt with will reveal the difference. The *Agni Purāṇa,* for instance, describes the mode of performance of a śrāddha in the following words:

After having invited brāhmaṇas the previous day, they

* See Appendices I and II.

should be welcomed in the afternoon, worshipped and seated on the seat. Two brāhmaṇas are invited in the ceremony intended for gods and one by one in the ceremony intended for departed forefathers. They are made to sit facing the east in the ceremony for the gods. There may be three or one brāhmaṇa in the ceremony for forefathers. The same procedure is followed in regard to the ceremonies of the maternal forefathers also. I shall describe the procedure for the vaiśvadeva. After having given waters for washing hands and kuśa grass for the sake of seat and having obtained permission from brāhmaṇas all gods should be invoked with the syllables, *viśve devāsaḥ*. After having spread the barley then, and pouring water in the vessel containing pavitraka (the purifying kuśa) with the syllables *śanno devīḥ* and then the barley with the syllables *yavo'si,* the libation is placed on the hand with the sacred syllables *yā divyā*. Then, after having offered waters, fragrance, flowers, incense and lamp, and shifted the sacred thread to rest on the right shoulder, the forefathers should be circumambulated. The forefathers should be invoked with the syllables *uśantastvā* extending two kuśa grass. After having been permitted by them, one should recite the syllable *ā yantu naḥ*.

Sesamum should be used in the place of barley. Respectful offering of water should be made as before. After having done it, the remains of libation should be collected in a vessel as laid down and the vessel is turned upside down with the syllable *pitṛbhyaḥ sthānamasi*. Then the cooked rice covered with ghī should be taken in hand and asked, "shall I offer it to the fire?". Being permitted to do so saying, "Do it", one should offer it to the fire as in the ceremony done for the manes. The remnants of offering should be given with devotion in vessels secured according to one's status or especially in silver vessels. After having offered food the vessel should be consecrated with the sacred syllable *pṛthivīpātraṁ*. Then the thumb of the brāhmaṇa should be placed therein with the recitation of the sacred syllable *idaṁ viṣṇuḥ*. After reciting Gāyatrī together with the vyāhṛtis and the hymn madhuvātā it should be stated 'eat comfortably'. They should also eat controlling their speech. They should be served the cooked rice and the clarified butter after the repetition of sacred syllable of purification. Then the cooked rice should be taken and shown and enquired: "Are you satisfied?". The remaining cooked rice should be scattered on the ground and water should be sprinkled one by one. The cooked rice that was scattered should be gathered together with sesamum and as in the case of the ceremony for the manes the balls of rice should be offered remaining facing the south in proximity of the place where the food was eaten by the brāhmaṇas.

It is done in the same way for the maternal forefathers also. Then water for sipping is offered. Then the words of benediction should be uttered. So also the undecaying waters should be offered. After having paid fees befitting one's capacity, the syllable *svadhā* should be pronounced. After having been permitted to say, the words *svapitṛbhyaḥ svadhā (svadhā* to my forefathers) should be said. When the brāhmaṇa says let *svadhā* be repeated, it should be done so. Then water should be sprinkled on the ground. Water should be offered with the repetition of the syllables *prīyantāṁ* or *viśve devāḥ*. After having said: "Let our donors, the Vedas and the progeny flourish. Let not our earnestness dwindle. Let us have plenty to give" and uttering sweet words the brāhmaṇas should be allowed to go. The satisfied manes should be bade adieu after repeating the syllable *vāje vāje*.

The vessel in which the remnants of libation had been poured earlier, that vessel of the manes should be made upright and the brāhmaṇas should be bade adieu after following them in such a way as circumambulating. After having eaten remnants of the food partaken by the forefathers, one should observe continence that night in the company of brāhmaṇas. After having done the circumambulation of the manes in the nāndī in connection with the impurity caused by the birth of a child, they should be worshipped with the balls of barley mixed with curd and fruit of jujube.

The ekoddiṣṭa ceremony is done without the worship of Viśvedevas. There should be only one libation and one purificatory rite. The offering should be made in the āvāhana fire without the instrumental syllable with the sacred thread lying on the right shoulder. One should say 'let you get up' in place of 'imperishable' and 'may you be satisfied' in place of bidding adieu to the manes in the former. They should say, "We are satisfied".

Four vessels containing fragrant waters and sesamum should be kept apart, the vessel of the dead person should be sprinkled with waters, the waters of libation from the vessels of the forefathers with the two sacred syllables beginning with *ye samānā*. The remaining acts should be done as before. When this ekoddiṣṭa becomes the sapiṇḍīkaraṇa it should be done adding the dead woman also. If the sapiṇḍīkaraṇa has to be performed for a dead person within a year after death, the food for him should be given to a brāhmaṇa the whole year together with a vessel filled with water.

The ceremony should be done on the day of death for every month in a year and should be done for every year as the food offered every month. The forefathers would be satisfied for a month with cooked rice and a year with pāyasa (sweet liquid made with flour, rice, sago etc.). So also the offer made on the thirteenth day in the asterism of Māgha in the rainy season would no doubt please the manes.

One who does the annual ceremony always makes grow the prosperity of his daughter, progeny, attendants, animals, chief among the sons, ghī, agriculture, trade, animals cloven-footed and not cloven-footed, sons possessing the lustre of Brahman, gold, silver and the excellence of the relatives. He will also get his desires fulfilled. The ceremony is to be done on all days from the first lunar day except the fourteenth day. The ceremony is to be done on that day (fourteenth) for the sake of those who were killed by weapons. One who does the ceremony as laid down gets heaven, progeny, radiance, valour, land, strength, excellence of sons, progeny with prosperity, importance, sons, unimpeded sovereignty, trade, lordship, unimpaired health, fame, absence of grief, excellent state, wealth, learning, the accomplishment of a physician, silver, cows, small cattle, horses and long life.

If the ceremony is done in the asterisms commencing with Kṛttikā and ending with Bharaṇi one gets all these desires fulfilled. The Vasus, Rudras, Ādityas, the deities in the form of manes get pleased with the men who satisfy the manes with the performance of ceremony. The forefathers being pleased confer on men long life, progeny, wealth, learning, heaven, liberation and comforts.

The purāṇic description of the śrāddha ceremonies is essentially the same as recorded in the *Gṛhyasūtras*. Hiraṇyakeśin's instructions in this regard may be considered typical. He begins with the time appropriate to the performance of the monthly śrāddha and goes on to describe its mode and procedure. On the new-moon day, he says, in the afternoon, or on days with an odd number in the dark fortnight the monthly śrāddha is performed.

Having prepared food for the fathers and having arranged southward-pointed darbha grass as seats for the brāhmaṇas whom he is going to invite, he invites an odd number of pure brāhmaṇas who are versed in the mantras, with no deficient limbs, who are not connected with him by consanguinity or by their gotra or by the mantras, such as his teacher or his pupils. In feeding them he should not look at any worldly purposes.

Having put wood on the fire and strewn southward-pointed and eastward-pointed darbha grass around it, having prepared the ājya in an ājya pot over which he has laid one purifier, having sprinkled water round the fire from right to left, and put a piece of udumbara wood on the fire, he sacrifices with the spoon called Darvi which is made of udumbara wood. Having performed the rites down to the ājyabhāga offerings, he suspends his sacrificial cord over his right shoulder and calls the fathers to his sacrifice with the verse, 'Come hither, O Fathers, friends of Soma, on your hidden, ancient paths, bestowing on us offspring and wealth and long life, a life of a hundred autumns.'

He sprinkles water in the same direction (i.e. towards the south) with the verse, 'Divine waters, send us Agni. May our fathers enjoy this sacrifice. May they who receive their nourishment every month bestow on us wealth with valiant heroes.' Having performed the rites down to the vyāhṛti oblations with his sacrificial cord over his left shoulder, he suspends it over his right shoulder and sacrifices with the following mantras:

'To Soma with the fathers, svadhā! Adoration!

'To Yama with the Aṅgiras and with the fathers, svadhā! Adoration!

'With the waters that spring in the east and those that come from the north: with the waters, the supporters of the whole world, I interpose another one between myself and my father. Svadhā! Adoration!

'I interpose another one through the mountains; I interpose through the wide earth; through the sky and the points of the horizon, through infinite bliss I interpose another one between myself and my grandfather. Svadhā! Adoration!

'I interpose another one through the seasons, through days and nights with the beautiful twilight. Through half-months and months I interpose another one between myself and my great-grandfather. Svadhā! Adoration!'

Then he sacrifices with their names: 'Svadhā! Adoration! Svadhā! Adoration!'

'Wherein my mother has done amiss, abandoning her duty towards her husband, may my father take that sperm as his own; may another one fall off from the mother. Svadhā! Adoration!'

In the same way a second and a third verse with the alteration of the mantra, 'Wherein my grandmother', 'Wherein my great-grandmother.'

'The fathers who are here and who are not here, and whom we know and whom we do not know: Agni, to thee they are known, how many they are, Jātavedas. May they enjoy what thou givest them in our oblation. Svadhā! Adoration! Your limb that this flesh-devouring Agni has burnt, leading you to the worlds of the fathers, Jātavedas, that I restore to you again. Unviolated with all your limbs arise, O fathers! Svadhā! Adoration! Carry the ājya, Jātavedas, to the fathers, where thou knowest them resting afar. May streams of ājya flow to them; may their wishes with all their desires be fulfilled! Svadhā! Adoration!' In the same way a second and a third verse with the alteration of the mantra, 'to the grandfathers', 'to the great-grandfathers.'

In the same way he sacrifices the food, altering the mantra, 'Carry the food, &c.' Then he sacrifices the sviṣṭakṛt oblation with the formula, 'To Agni kavyavāhana sviṣṭakṛt svadhā! Adoration!' He then touches the food with the formulas, 'The earth is thy vessel, the heaven is the lid. I sacrifice thee into the Brahman's mouth. I sacrifice thee into the up-breathing and down-breathing of the brāhmaṇas. Thou art imperishable; do not perish for the fathers yonder, in yon world! The earth is steady; Agni is its surveyor in order that what has been given may not be lost.

'The earth is thy vessel, the heaven is the lid, &c. Do not perish for the grandfathers yonder, in yon world. The air is steady; Vāyu is its surveyor, in order that what has been given may not be lost. The earth is thy vessel, the heaven is the lid. Do not perish for the great-grandfathers yonder, in yon world. The heaven is steady; Āditya is its surveyor, in order that what has been given may not be lost.' With the words, 'I establish myself in the breath and sacrifice ambrosia', he causes the brāhmaṇas to touch the food.

While they are eating, he looks at them with the words, 'My soul (ātman) dwells in Brahman that it may be immortal.' When they have eaten and go away, he goes after them and asks for their permission to take the remains of their meal for the rites which he is going to perform. Then he takes a water-pot and a handful of darbha grass, goes forth to a place that lies in a south-easterly intermediate direction, spreads the darbha grass out with its points towards the south, and pours out on that grass with downward-turned hands, ending in the south, three handfuls of water, with the formulas, 'May the fathers, the friends of Soma, wipe themselves! May the grandfathers . . . the great-grandfathers, the friends of Soma, wipe themselves!' Wash thyself! Wash thyself!

On that grass he puts down, with downward-turned hands, ending in the south, the lumps of food for the fathers. To his father he gives his lump with the words, 'This to thee, father', to the grandfather with the words, 'This to thee, grandfather', to the great-grandfather with the words, 'This to thee, great-grandfather', silently a fourth lump. This fourth lump is optional. Should he not know the names of the ancestors, he gives the lump to the father with the words, 'Svadhā to the fathers who dwell on the earth', to the grandfather with the words, 'Svadhā to the fathers who dwell in the air', to the great-grandfather with the words, 'Svadhā to the fathers who dwell in heaven.'

Then he gives, corresponding to each lump, collyrium

and other salve and something that represents a garment. The collyrium he gives, saying three times, 'Anoint thy eyes! Anoint thy eyes!' The salve, saying three times, 'Anoint thyself, Anoint thyself!' With the formula, 'These garments are for you, O fathers. Do not seize upon anything else that is ours', he tears off a skirt of his garment or a flake of wool and puts that down for the fathers, if he is in the first half of his life. He tears out some hairs of his body, if in the second half.

Then he washes the vessel in which the food was of which he had offered the lumps, and sprinkles the water with which he has washed it, from right to left round the lumps with the mantra, 'These honey-sweet waters, bringing refreshment to children and grandchildren, giving sweet drink and ambrosia to the fathers, the divine waters refresh both the living and the dead, these rivers, abounding in water, covered with reeds, with beautiful bathing-places; may they flow up to you in yon world!' Then he turns the vessel over, crosses his hands so that the left hand becomes right and the right hand becomes left, and worships the fathers with the formulas of adoration, 'Adoration to you, O fathers, for the sake of sap.'

Then he goes to the brink of some water and pours down three handfuls of water with the following mantras:

'This is for thee, father, this honey-sweet wave, rich in water. As great as Agni and the earth are, so great is its measure, so great is its might. As such a great one I give it. As Agni is imperishable and inexhaustible, thus may it be imperishable and inexhaustible, sweet drink to my father. By that imperishable wave, that sweet drink, live thou together with those. The *ṛcās* are thy might. This is for thee, great-grandfather. . . As great as Āditya and the heaven are . . . The sāmans are thy might'.

Returning from the place where he has performed the piṇḍa offerings he puts the substance cleaving to the sthālī into the water-pot and pours it out, with the verse, 'Go away, O fathers, friends of Soma, on your hidden, ancient paths. After a month return again to our house and eat our offerings, rich in offspring, in valiant sons.' Thereby the śrāddha celebrated in the middle of the rainy season has been declared.

Hiraṇyakeśin now explains the festival of the Aṣṭakā. The eighth day of the dark fortnight that follows after the full moon of Māgha, is called Ekāṣṭakā. On the day before that Aṣṭakā, under the nakṣatra Anurādhā, in the afternoon he puts wood on the fire, strews southward-pointed and eastward-pointed darbha grass around it, and turns rice out of four shallow cups over which he has laid one purifier, with the mantra, 'I turn out, impelled by the god Sāvitrī, this cake prepared from four cups of rice, which may drive away all suffering from the fathers in the other world. On the impulse of the god Sāvitrī, with the arms of the two Aśvins, with Pūṣan's hands I turn thee out, agreeable to the fathers, the grandfathers, the great-grandfathers.'

With the same purifier he silently strains the prokṣaṇī water; he silently sprinkles with that water the rice and the vessels, silently husks the rice, silently bakes it in four dishes like a puroḍāśa, sprinkles ājya on it, takes it from the fire, sprinkles water round the fire from right to left, and puts a piece of udumbara wood on the fire. With the spoon called darvi which is made of udumbara wood, he cuts off in one continual line which is directed towards south-east, the avadāna portions one after the other, spreading under and sprinkling over them ājya, and sacrifices them, one after the other, in one continual line which is directed towards south-east, with the mantras, 'The mortars, the pressing-stones have made their noise, preparing the annual offering. Ekāṣṭakā! May we be rich in offspring, in valiant sons, the Lords of wealth. Svadhā! Adoration!

'God Agni! The cake which is prepared with ghī and accompanied by the word svadhā, that the fathers may satiate themselves—this our offering carry duly, Agni. I, the son, sacrifice an oblation to my fathers. Svadhā! Adoration! Here is a cake, Agni, prepared from four cups of rice, with ghī, rich in milk, in wealth, in prosperity. May the fathers gladly accept it all together; may it be well sacrificed and well offered by me. Svadhā! Adoration!'

Then he makes oblations of other food with the verses, 'The one who shone forth as the first', 'The Ekāṣṭakā, devoting herself to austerities', 'She who shone forth as the first'.

Cutting off the avadānas destined for the sviṣṭakṛt oblation together from the cake and from the other food and mixing them with clarified butter, he makes an oblation thereof with the formula, 'To Agni kavyavāhana sviṣṭakṛt svadhā! Adoration!' That cake with ghī and honey and with the food mentioned in the *Sūtras*, he touches in the way prescribed for the śrāddha ceremony and puts down lumps of it according to the ritual of the piṇḍa offerings. The remains of that cake, &c. he serves to learned brāhmaṇas. He gives them food and presents as at the śrāddha ceremony. The known rites down to the pouring out of the handfuls of water are performed here as at the monthly śrāddha.

On the following day he sacrifices a cow to the fathers. Having put wood on the fire and strewn southward-pointed and eastward-pointed darbha grass around it, he sacrifices the oblation for the touching of the animal with the verse, 'This cow I touch for the fathers; may my assembled fathers gladly accept it which is offered with ghī, with the word svadhā; may it satiate my fathers in the other world. Svadhā! Adoration!' Then he touches the cow with one blade of sacrificial grass and with an unforked vapāśrapaṇī of udumbara wood, with the formula, 'I touch thee agreeable to the fathers.'

The sacrifice of the cow is essoterical. By honouring the cow ceremoniously and then letting go free to roam, one reaps bliss in abundance.

The *Gṛhyasūtra* of Āpastamba devotes three sections (21-23, Paṭala 8) to the mode of performing the monthly śrāddha. In his brief comments on the ritual, he says that the times for them are in the second fortnight of the month. The performer is asked to feed without regard of worldly purposes, the pure brāhmaṇas, versed in the mantras, who are not connected with him by consanguinity or by their gotra or by the mantras such as his teacher or his pupils, an odd number, at least three.

He makes oblations of the food prepared for the brāhmaṇas with the next verses, II, 19, 1-7. Then the ājya oblations indicated by the next mantras, II, 19, 8-13. Or invertedly, i.e. he offers ājya with the verses referred to in sūtra 3, and food with those referred to in sūtra 4. Let him touch the whole food with the next formulas, II, 19, 14-16. Or the single prepared portions of food destined for the single brāhmaṇa. Having caused them with the next formula, II, 20, 1 to touch the food, he gives it to them to eat.

When they have eaten and gone away, he goes after them, circumambulates them, turning his right side towards them, spreads out southward-pointed darbha grass in two different layers, pours water on it with the next formulas, II, 20, 2-7, distributes the piṇḍas, ending in the south, with the next formulas, II, 20, 8-13, pours out water as before with the next formulas, 14-19, worships the ancestors with the next formulas, II, 20, 20-23, sprinkles with the next verse, (24) water three times from right to left round the piṇḍas with a water-pot, besprinkles the vessels, which are turned upside down, repeating the next yajus (25) at least three times without taking breath, sets up the vessels two by two, cuts off avadānas from all portions of food, and eats of the remains at least one morsel with the next yajus (26).

Of the dark fortnight that follows after the full moon of Māgha, the eighth day falls under the constellation of Jyeṣṭhā: this day is called Ekāṣṭakā. In the evening before that day he performs the preparatory ceremony. He bakes a cake of four cups of rice. The cake is prepared in eight dishes like a puroḍāśa, according to some teachers.

After the ceremonies down to the ājyabhāga oblations have been performed in the same way as at the fortnightly sacrifices, he makes with his joined hands oblations of the cake with the next verse, II, 20, 27. The rest of the cake he makes ready, divides it into eight parts and offers it to the brāhmaṇas. On the following day he touches a cow with a darbha blade, with the words, 'I touch thee agreeable to the fathers.'

The rites from the sviṣṭakṛt down to the offering of the piṇḍas are the same as at the śrāddha. Some teachers prescribe the piṇḍa offering for the day after the Aṣṭakā. Here follows another way for celebrating the Aṣṭakā sacrifice. He sacrifices curds with his joined hands in the same way as the cake.

If he goes out in order to beg for something, let him murmur the next mantras, II, 21, 10-16 and then state his desire. If he has obtained a chariot, he has the horses put to it, lets it face the east, and touches with the next verse, II, 21, 17 the two wheels of the chariot or the two side-pieces. With the next yajus II, 21, 18 he should mount, and drive with the next verse, II, 21, 19 towards the east or north, and should then drive off on his business. Let him mount a horse with the next formulas, II, 21, 20-30; an elephant with the next formula, II, 21, 31. If any harm is done him by these two beasts, let him touch the earth as indicated above. If he is going to a dispute, he takes the parasol and the staff in his left hand.

Having sacrificed, with his right hand, a fist full of chaff with the next verse, II, 21, 32, he should go away and murmur the next verse, 33. Over an angry person let him recite the two next formulas, II, 22, 1-2; then his anger will be appeased.

For success in trade let him sacrifice with the next verse, II, 22, 4—some portion from the articles of trade which he has in his house.

In a path which servants or labourers use to run away, he should put plates used for protecting the hands when holding a hot sacrificial pan on a fire, and should offer the oblations indicated by the next mantras, II, 22, 7-10. If a fruit falls on him from a tree, or a bird befouls him, or a drop of water falls on him when no rain is expected, he should wipe that off with the next mantras, II, 22, 11-13, according to the characteristics contained in these mantras.

If a post of his house puts forth shoots, or if honey is made in his house by bees, or if the footprint of a dove is seen on the hearth, or if diseases arise in his household, or in the case of other miracles or prodigies, let him perform in the new-moon night, at the dead of night, at a place where he does not hear the noise of water, the rites from the putting of wood on the fire down to the ājyabhāga oblations, and let him offer the oblations indicated in the next mantras, II, 22, 14-23, and enter upon the performance of the Gayā and following oblations. Having performed the ceremonies down to the sprinkling of water round the fire, he puts up towards the south with the next verse, II, 22, 24 a stone as a barrier for those among whom a death has occurred.

The foregoing descriptions are indeed valuable for one desirous of performing the monthly and annual śrāddha performed at the crematorium and at the home of the deceased by his son or one authorised by the law books to perform it. Considerable importance is attached to this first śrāddha. The monthly and the annual śrāddhas, though important, may be said to hold a secondary position, much less a vital one, to the living progeny of the dead.

THE ANTYEṢṬI SAṀSKĀRA
(The Hindu Obsequial Rites)

The law-books describe the last rites at considerable length, often designating them as antyeṣṭi saṁskāra or obsequial ceremonies or funeral rites. These are performed with great pomp and ceremony in the event of a person dying in old age and with all possible gravity and seriousness if one dies in youth. Considering the human body to be frail and evanescent, most people perform the last rites with stoic resignation and as one of the principal saṁskāras. The crying and wailing of the mourners are of no avail once a kinsman dies, instead they make one inconsolable and inexpressibly sad. The śāstras, therefore, forbid valedicatory mourning:

रोदनापेक्षया कुर्यात् सुव्यवस्थां मृतात्मनः।
समाश्रितासमर्थानां पुत्रादीनां समाचरेत् ॥
कल्याणमयकर्माणि मृतात्मनः सुशान्तये ।
तच्छेषोत्तरदायित्वं विदधेच्च शुभेच्छया ॥

rodanāpekṣayā kuryāt suvyavasthāṁ mṛtātmanaḥ ।
samāśritāsamarthānāṁ putrādīnāṁ samācaret ॥
kalyāṇamayakarmāṇi mṛtātmanaḥ suśāntaye ।
taccheṣottaradāyitvaṁ vidadhecca śubhecchayā ॥

It would be better, says the seer here, to look after the dependents of the dead than to cry over spilt milk. The wise prefer doing what they can for the well-being of the needy so that the souls of the dead may rest in peace; they dedicate their lives to the fulfilment of the tasks left unfinished by the deceased.

Of men, there are very few who remember their duties

at the time of death and fewer still who renounce all attachment and their sense of tasks unfulfilled. At such moments the kinsfolk of the dying man have a bounden duty, mainly, to sustain his drooping spirit and not to give way to a tearful grief. It would be depressing for a man about to breathe his last to find people wailing around his death-bed. It is, therefore, incumbent upon the living to encourage him by reading the scriptures aloud and, if possible, hymning prayers to his chosen deity. Those near the dying man should discuss scriptural episodes from the *Rāmāyaṇa*, the *Gītā* and the *Bhāgavata*. The impatient man, who earned during his lifetime full-throated praise for his valiant optimism, must not be allowed to yield to disconsolation and to lose heart.

One of the notable instructions given by the seers is that the dying man should offer a gift or two with his own hand for his own well-being. Gifts are stated to be of various kinds—the gift of foodgrains, the gift of a cow, of land, gold, precious stones, etc. The object offered must be in keeping with one's faith. The scholar-pandits are of the view that the gift of a cow made by the dying is the most salutary and supremely desirable. Another piece of instruction given by the śāstras is that the wishes of the dying in respect of the gifts to be offered must be honoured, though in no case should one be so blind as to lose his sense of proportion or of his financial means. This is the most proper occasion when the well-wishers of the dying repeat such redemptive mantras as the Gāyatrī and the Mahāmṛtyuñjaya with due solemnity and in accordance with the instructions laid down in the law books. On realizing that death is now imminent within an hour or so, let the ground be smeared with cowdung and the dying be laid there on kuśa blades and a woollen blanket. His head should lie in the southern direction. As another redemptive measure, let the verses from the *Gītā*, the *Rāmāyaṇa* etc. continue to be chanted as long as the dying man is not declared dead.

The Hindu book of the dead ordains that before the last summons comes and the man on the death-bed is felt to be collapsing, his head should be turned to the north and feet to the south. Drop a little clarified butter into the eyes and ears of the dead and cover the corpse with a piece of cloth. This is followed by bathing and clothing it according to the family custom and then laying it down on the bier. All this is done according to different customs prevailing in different countries.

Funeral Procession

The person who is authorised to light the funeral pyre should, before performing the last rites, have his hair shaved and then, after a purificatory bath, change his clothes. He should then sit to the right of corpse with his sacred thread hanging from the right shoulder to the left side. It is thus that he should offer the piṇḍa* with saṁkalpa or resolution to perform the rites according to the scriptural injunctions, he should place the piṇḍas on the bosom of the corpse or on its either side. The piṇḍas should be made of barley flour mixed with sesamum, clarified butter and jaggery. The number of the piṇḍas can vary from twenty-four to six according to the custom in vogue where the rite is being performed. The most common and widespread saṁkalpa for the offering of the piṇḍas is as follows:

अद्य (अमुक) गोत्रस्य (अमुक) प्रेतस्य प्रेततानिवृत्त्यर्थं उत्तमलोके प्राप्त्यर्थं और्ध्वदैहिककर्म करिष्ये ।

adya (amuka) gotrasya (amuka) pretasya pretatānivṛtt-yartham uttamaloke prāptyartham aurdhvadaihikakarma kariṣye ।

---

* A ball of rice or flour offered to the pitṛs or deceased ancestors.

A variant of this custom is to make offerings of piṇḍas; then the bier is carried out of doors. Thereupon the kinsfolk, the members of the family, relatives and friends follow the bier to the cremation ground. Yet another variant is to offer the piṇḍas at crossroads and at all those places where the bier is kept to rest before reaching the crematorium. The leg-side of the bier should lead till it reaches the place of rest. But from here onwards the bier turns round and the head begins to lead. Where this practice is reversed, people are advised to follow their own traditional customs.

On reaching the crematorium, have the ground for the funeral pyre cleansed and smeared with cowdung. With a view to making it thoroughly clean befitting the solemnity of the ritual, also recite the following mantra:

ॐ शुद्धवालः सर्वशुद्धवालो मणिवालस्तऽआश्विनाः श्येतः श्येताक्षोऽरुणस्ते रुद्राय पशुपतये कर्णा यामाऽअवलिप्ता रौद्रा नभोरूपाः पार्जन्याः ॥

Om śuddhavālaḥ sarvaśuddhavālo maṇivālasta' āśvināḥ śyetaḥ syetākṣo' ruṇaste rudrāya paśupataye karṇā yāmā' avaliptā raudrā nabhorūpāḥ pārjanyāḥ ॥

Having sprinkled the ground with water sanctified by sacred formulas, indite 'om' on it and scatter a little sesamum seeds, etc. all around it. The mantra relevant to this occasion is as follows:

ॐ ओमासश्चर्षणीधृतो विश्वे देवास आगत । दाश्वा ꣹ सो दाशुषः सुतम् । उपयामगृहीतोऽसि विश्वेभ्यस्त्वा देवेभ्यः । एष ते योनिर्विश्वेभ्यस्त्वा देवेभ्यः ॥

om omāsaścarṣaṇīdhṛto viśve devāsa'āgata । dāśvāṁso dāśuṣaḥ sutam । upayāmagṛhīto'si viśvebhyastvā devebhyaḥ । eṣa te yonirviśvebhyastvā devebhyaḥ ॥

Having hymned this, collect an adequate quantity of easily inflammable wood for the funeral. As the corpse is laid down with its feet towards the north, pour a little clarified butter into his nose, ears and eyes. It should also be noted that all around the funeral pyre erected on the cremation ground, four pieces of wood (samidhās) are kept as symbols of an altar. While keeping the firewood in every direction, the following mantras should be chanted:

पूर्व– ॐ प्राची दिगग्निरधिपतिरसितो रक्षितादित्या इषवः । तेभ्यो नमोऽधिपतिभ्यो नमो रक्षितृभ्यो नम इषुभ्यो नम एभ्यो अस्तु । योऽस्मान्द्वेष्टि यं वयं द्विष्मस्तं वो जम्भे दध्मः ॥

दक्षिण– ॐ दक्षिणा दिगिन्द्रोऽधिपतिस्तिरश्चिराजी रक्षिता पितर इषवः तेभ्यो नमोऽधिपतिभ्यो नमो रक्षितृभ्यो नम इषुभ्यो नम एभ्यो अस्तु । योऽस्मान्द्वेष्टि यं वयं द्विष्मस्तं वो जम्भे दध्मः ॥

पश्चिम– ॐ प्रतीची दिग्वरुणोऽधिपतिः पृदाकू रक्षिताऽन्नमिषवः । तेभ्यो नमोऽधिपतिभ्यो नमो रक्षितृभ्यो नम इषुभ्यो नमः एभ्यो अस्तु । योऽस्मान् द्वेष्टि यं वयं द्विष्मस्तं वो जम्भे दध्मः ॥

उत्तर– ॐ उदीची दिक् सोमोऽधिपतिः स्वजो रक्षिता शनिरिषवः । तेभ्यो नमोऽधिपतिभ्यो नमो रक्षितृभ्यो नम इषुभ्यो नम एभ्यो अस्तु । योऽस्मान् द्वेष्टि यं वयं द्विष्मस्तं वो जम्भे दध्मः ॥

East : om prācī digagniradhipatirasito rakṣitādityā iṣavaḥ I tebhyo namo'dhipatibhyo namo rakṣitṛbhyo nama iṣubhyo nama ebhyo astu I yo'smāndveṣṭi yaṁ vayaṁ dviṣmastaṁ vo jambhe dadhmaḥ II

South : om dakṣiṇā digindro'dhipatistiraścirājī rakṣitā pitara iṣavaḥ tebhyo namo 'dhipatibhyo namo rakṣitṛbhyo nama iṣubhyo nama ebhyo astu I yo'smāndveṣṭi yaṁ vayaṁ dviṣmastaṁ vo jambhe dadhmaḥ II

West : om pratīcī digvaruṇo'dhipatiḥ pṛdākū ra-

kṣitā'nnamiṣavaḥ I tebhyo namo'dhipatibhyo namo rakṣitṛbhyo nama iṣubhyo namaḥ ebhyo astu I yo'smān dveṣṭi yaṁ vayaṁ dviṣmastaṁ vo jambhe dadhmaḥ II

North : *om udīcī dik somo'dhipatiḥ svajo rakṣitā śanirisavaḥ I tebhyo namo'dhipatibhyo namo rakṣitṛbhyo nama iṣubhyo nama ebhyo astu I yo'smān dveṣṭi yaṁ vayaṁ dviṣmastaṁ vo jambhe dadhmaḥ II*

Before the corpse is kept on the pyre, bathe it and then sprinkle a little water on it with kuśa blades as you read the following mantra:

ॐ आपो हि ष्ठा मयोभुवस्ता ना ऊर्जे दधातन । ॐ महे रणाय चक्षसे । ॐ यो वः शिवतमो रसस्तस्य भाजयतेह नः । ॐ उशतीरिव मातरः । ॐ तस्मा अरं गमाम वो यस्य क्षयाय जिन्वथ । ॐ आपो जनयथा च नः ॥

om āpo hi ṣṭhā mayobhuvastā nā ūrje dadhātana I om mahe raṇāya cakṣase I om yo vaḥ śivatamo rasastasya bhājayateha naḥ I om uśatīriva mātaraḥ I om tasmā araṁ gamāma vo yasya kṣayāya jinvatha I om āpo janayathā ca naḥ II

It is only then that the corpse, already sanctified by mantras, is laid on the pyre and the following mantra is chanted:

ॐ अग्ने नय सुपथा राये अस्मान् विश्वानि देव वयुनानि विद्वान् ।
युयोध्यस्मज्जुहुराणमेनो भूयिष्ठां ते नम उक्तिं विधेम ॥

om agne naya supathā rāye asmān viśvāni deva vayunāni vidvān I
yuyodhyasmajjuhurāṇameno bhūyiṣṭhāṁ te nama uktiṁ vidhema II

The Cremation

Having kept the corpse on the pyre with the above

mantra, let some more pieces of firewood be added to it. The next step is to perform the pañcabhūsaṁskāra* towards the head on a piece of ground duly cleansed and purified. Then, uttering 'क्रव्यादाय नमः' (kravyādāya namaḥ) light the fire called Kravyāda** (क्रव्याद) and then keep it on the funeral pyre with the following mantra:

> ॐ भूर्भुवः स्वर्द्यौरिव भूम्ना पृथिवीव वरिम्णा ।
> तस्यास्ते पृथिवि देवयजनि पृष्ठेऽग्निमन्नादमन्नाद्यायादधे ।
> अग्निं दूतं पुरो दधे हव्यवाहमुपब्रुवे । देवाँआ सादयादिह ॥
> *om bhūrbhuvaḥ svar dyauriva bhūmnā pṛthivīva varimṇā । tasyāste pṛthivi devayajani pṛṣṭhe'gnimannādamannādyāyādadhe । agniṁ dūtaṁ puro dadhe havyavāhamupabruve । devāṁā sādayādiha ॥*

Thereafter make seven fire offerings one after another as you do when performing Agnihotra (oblation to Firegod). Each offering should be made with a separate mantra:

> ॐ प्रजापतये स्वाहा, इदं प्रजापतये न मम ॥१॥
> ॐ इन्द्राय स्वाहा, इदमिन्द्राय न मम ॥२॥
> ॐ अग्नये स्वाहा, इदमग्नये न मम ॥३॥
> ॐ सोमाय स्वाहा, इदं सोमाय न मम ॥४॥
> ॐ यमाय स्वाहा, इदं यमाय न मम ॥५॥
> ॐ मृत्यवे स्वाहा, इदं मृत्यवे न मम ॥६॥
> ॐ ब्रह्मणे स्वाहा, इदं ब्रह्मणे न मम ॥७॥
> *om prajāpataye svāhā, idaṁ prajāpataye na mama ॥1॥*
> *om indrāya svāhā, idamindrāya na mama ॥2॥*
> *om agnaye svāhā, idamagnaye na mama ॥3॥*
> *om somāya svāhā, idaṁ somāya na mama ॥4॥*
> *om yamāya svāhā, idaṁ yamāya na mama ॥5॥*
> *om mṛtyave svāhā, idaṁ mṛtyave na mama ॥6॥*
> *om brahmaṇe svāhā, idaṁ brahmaṇe na mama ॥7॥*

---

* See Appendix III.

** The fire of the funeral pile.

Next, offer three oblations seriatim to the *vyāhṛtis* with the following mantras:

ॐ भूः स्वाहा, इदमग्नये न मम ॥१॥
ॐ भुवः स्वाहा, इदं वायवे न मम ॥२॥
ॐ स्वः स्वाहा, इदं सूर्याय न मम ॥३॥
om bhūḥ svāhā, idamagnaye na mama ॥1॥
om bhuvaḥ svāhā, idaṁ vāyave na mama ॥2॥
om svaḥ svāhā, idaṁ sūryāya na mama ॥3॥

It may be pointed out that *vyāhṛti* is utterance of the names of the seven worlds (*viz.,* bhūr, bhuvar or bhuvaḥ, svar, mahar, janar, tapas, satya), the first three of which, called the great vyāhṛtis, are pronounced after *OM* by every brāhmaṇa in commencing his daily prayers and are personified as the daughters of Sāvitrī and Pṛśni.

Such oblations are offered as dedication of every physical organ to the Fire-god (Agni):

ॐ लोमभ्यः स्वाहा, इदं लोमभ्यो न मम ॥१॥
ॐ त्वचे स्वाहा, इदं त्वचे न मम ॥२॥
ॐ लोहिताय स्वाहा, इदं लोहिताय न मम ॥३॥
ॐ मेदोभ्यः स्वाहा, इदं मेदोभ्यो न मम ॥४॥
ॐ मांसेभ्यः स्वाहा, इदं मांसेभ्यो न मम ॥५॥
ॐ स्नायुभ्यः स्वाहा, इदं स्नायुभ्यो न मम ॥६॥
ॐ अस्थिभ्यः स्वाहा, इदं अस्थिभ्यो न मम ॥७॥
ॐ मज्जाभ्यः स्वाहा, इदं मज्जाभ्यो न मम ॥८॥
ॐ रेतसे स्वाहा, इदं रेतसे न मम ॥९॥
ॐ पायवे स्वाहा, इदं पायवे न मम ॥१०॥
om lomabhyaḥ svāhā, idaṁ lomabhyo na mama ॥1॥
om tvace svāhā, idaṁ tvace na mama ॥2॥
om lohitāya svāhā, idaṁ lohitāya na mama ॥3॥
om medobhyaḥ svāhā, idaṁ medobhyo na mama ॥4॥
om māṁsebhyaḥ svāhā, idaṁ māṁsebhyo na mama ॥5॥
om snāyubhyaḥ svāhā, idaṁ snāyubhyo na mama ॥6॥

om asthibhyaḥ svāhā, idaṁ asthibhyo na mama ॥7॥
om majjābhayaḥ svāhā, idaṁ majjābhyo na mama ॥8॥
om retase svāhā, idaṁ retase na mama ॥9॥
om pāyave svāhā, idaṁ pāyave na mama ॥10॥

With the chanting of the following offer five oblations with fire and ghī:

ॐ आयुर्यज्ञेन कल्पताम् प्राणो यज्ञेन कल्पताञ्चक्षुर्यज्ञेन कल्पतां श्रोत्रं यज्ञेन कल्पतां वाग्यज्ञेन कल्पतां मनो यज्ञेन कल्पतामात्मा यज्ञेन कल्पतां ब्रह्मा यज्ञेन कल्पतां ज्योतिर्यज्ञेन कल्पतां स्वर्यज्ञेन कल्पतां पृष्ठं यज्ञेन कल्पतां यज्ञो यज्ञेन कल्पतां स्वाहा ॥
om āyuryajñena kalpatāṁ prāṇo yajñena kalpatāñcakṣuryajñena kalpatāṁ śrotraṁ yajñena kalpatāṁ vāgyajñena kalpatāṁ mano yajñena kalpatāmātmā yajñena kalpatāṁ brahma yajñena kalpatāṁ jyotiryajñena kalpatāṁ svaryajñena kalpatāṁ pṛṣṭhaṃ yajñena kalpatāṁ yajño yajñena kalpatāṁ svāhā ॥

Prior to this, the fifth piṇḍa called Sādhaka, is offered to the funeral pyre followed by going around the corpse and then lighting the fire in the manner indicated above. At the end offer oblations of clarified butter five times each with a Gāyatrī mantra.

ॐ भूर्भुवः स्वः तत्सवितुर्वरेण्यं भर्गोदेवस्य धीमहि । धियो यो नः प्रचोदयात् ॥
om bhūrbhuvaḥ svaḥ tatsviturvareṇyaṁ bhargo devasya dhīmahi । *dhiyo yo naḥ pracodayāt* ॥

Kapālakriyā

This is said to be the last funeral rite and is also called 'Mastakachedana'. As a matter of fact, this rite generally resembles the ultimate (complete) oblation (pūrṇāhuti) offered in a sacrifice. Just as one makes a hole in the hard hairy shell of a coconut and fills it with clarified butter, so in the corpse's head is bored a hole and filled with sesamum and ghṛta. Thus ends the last rite with the following mantra:

असौ स्वर्गाय लोकाय स्वाहा ज्वलतु पावके ।

asau svargāya lokāya svāhā jvalatu pāvake ।

Prolonging the ritual of kapālakriyā, some people also let a stream of clarified butter be poured on the funeral pyre as the last oblation. If this custom is adopted, read the following when letting the ghṛta stream forth:

ॐ वसोः पवित्रमसि शतधारं वसो पवित्रमसि सहस्त्रधारम् । देवस्त्वा सविता पुनातु वसो पवित्रेण शतधारेण सुप्वा कामधुक् स्वाहा ॥

om vasoḥ pavitramasi śatadhāraṁ vaso pavitramasi sahasradhāram । devastvā savitā punātu vaso pavitreṇa śatadhāreṇa supvā kāmadhuk svāhā ॥

The obsequial rites completed, wash the funeral ground clean with water. Some pious souls, not content with consigning the dead to the flames, gather the unburnt bones of the dead to throw them into the sacred rivers like the Gaṅgā. The last act, which is performed by the member who has lighted the pyre, is to take purificatory bath with the following mantra:

ॐ अप नः शोशुचदघमग्ने शुशुग्ध्या रयिम् । अप नः शोशुचदघम् ।

om apa naḥ śośucadaghamagne śuśugdhyā rayim ।
apa naḥ śośucadagham ॥

The bath being over, wear fresh clothes and then, having done the ācamana (sipping water), offer tilāñjali (a handful of water mixed with sesamum seeds offered to the deceased ancestors). Alternatively, let barley and sesamum seeds be mixed up and thrown into the water. The curtain falls here and the mourners, some extremely disconsolate and inconsolable, return home often with eyes streaming with tears.

Postmortem Rituals

Obsequial rites end here. Other rites related to and constituting an integral part of these rites, such as asthisaṁcaya (collection of bones), tṛtīya, navarātra or daśarātra, ekādaśāha sapiṇḍīkaraṇa, etc. are performed later. These are postmortem saṁskāras. The mantras intoned in all these rituals may now be stated for the convenience of the performers.

Before the rites begin to be performed, it is the duty of the ācārya to make his host utter the following saṁkalpa. Having mentioned his nationality and time, the host should thus speak:

अमुकगोत्रोत्पन्न अमुकशर्मा (वर्मा, गुप्तः) अहं श्रीपरमेश्वरप्रीत्यर्थे अमुकस्य मरणोत्तरं च देवऋषिपितृतर्पणं करिष्ये ।
amukagotrotpanna amukaśarmā (varmā, guptaḥ) ahaṁ śrīparameśvaraprītyarthe amukasya maraṇottaraṁ ca devarṣipitṛtarpaṇaṁ kariṣye ।

It should be noted that the manes are the presiding deities in these rites. It is desirable, therefore, to invoke the manes with the following:

ओ३म् विश्वेदेवास आगत शृणुता म इमं हवम् । इदं बर्हिर्निषीदत ॥
om viśvedevāsa āgata śṛṇutā ma imaṃ havam । *idaṁ barhirniṣīdata* ॥

Pañcabali (five propitiatory offerings)

Even before the manes are invoked, food, kept apart for different beings, is called Pañcabali. Separate mantras should be chanted for making offerings to the cow, the dog, the crow, the deities and the ant. These are as follows:

गोबलि - ओ३म् सौरभेय्यः सर्वहिताः पवित्राः पुण्यराशयः । प्रतिगृह्णन्तु मे ग्रासं गावस्त्रैलोक्यमातरः। इदं गोभ्यो न मम ॥

श्वानबलि -	ॐ द्वौ श्वानौ श्यामसबलौ वैवस्वतकुलोद्भवौ । ताभ्यामन्नं प्रदास्यामि स्यातामेतावहिंसकौ ॥ इदं श्वभ्यां न मम ॥
काकबलि -	ॐ ऐन्द्रवारुणवायव्या याम्या वै नैर्ऋतास्तथा । वायसाःप्रतिगृह्णन्तु भूमौ पिण्डं मयार्पितम् । इदं वायसेभ्यो न मम ॥
देवादिबलि -	ॐ देवा मनुष्याः पशवो वयांसि सिद्धाश्च यक्षोरगदैत्यसंघाः । प्रेताः पिशाचास्तरवः समस्ता ये चान्नमिच्छन्ति मया प्रदत्तम् ॥ इदमन्नं देवादिभ्यो न मम ॥
पिपीलिकाबलि-	ॐ पिपीलिकाः कीटपतंगकाद्या बुभुक्षिताः कर्मनिबन्धबद्धाः। तेषां हि तृप्त्यर्थमिदं मयान्नं तेभ्यो विसृष्टं सुखिनो भवन्तु ॥ इदमन्नं पिपीलिकादिभ्यो न मम ॥
gobali-	*om saurabheyyaḥ sarvahitāḥ pavitrāḥ puṇyarāśayaḥ । pratigṛhṇantu me grāsaṁ gāvastrailokyamātaraḥ । idaṁ gobhyo na mama* ॥
śvānabali-	*om dvau śvānau śyāmasabalau vaivasvatakulodbhavau । tābhyāmannaṁ pradāsyāmi syātāmetāvahiṁsakau ॥ idaṁ śvabhyāṁ na mama* ॥
kākabali-	*om aindravāruṇavāyavyā yāmyā vai nairṛtāstathā । vāyasāḥ pratigṛhṇantu bhūmau piṇḍaṁ mayārpitam । idaṁ vāyasebhyo na mama* ॥
devādibali-	*om devā manuṣyāḥ paśavo vayāṁsi siddhāśca yakṣoragadaityasaṁghāḥ । pretāḥ piśācāstaravaḥ samastā ye cānnamicchanti mayā pradattam ॥ idamannaṁ devādibhyo na mama* ॥
pipīlikābali-	*om pipīlikāḥ kīṭapataṁgakādyā bubhuk-*

ṣitāḥ karmanibandhabaddhāḥ । teṣāṁ hi tṛptyarthamidaṁ mayānnaṁ tebhyo visṛṣṭaṁ sukhino bhavantu ॥ idamannaṁ pipīlikādibhyo na mama ॥

Pitṛbali

For offerings to the pitṛs food should be kept on a leafy platter and offered to them with the following sacred formula:

ॐ नमो वः पितरो रसाय नमो वः पितरः शोषाय नमो वः पितरो जीवाय नमो वः पितरः स्वधायै नमो वः पितरो घोराय नमो वः पितरो मन्यवे नमो वः पितरः पितरो नमो वो व गृहान्नः पितरो दत्त सतो वः पितरो देष्मैतद् वः पितरो वासः ॥

om namo vaḥ pitaro rasāya namo vaḥ pitaraḥ śoṣāya namo vaḥ pitaro jīvāya namo vaḥ pitaraḥ svadhāyai namo vaḥ pitaro ghorāya namo vaḥ pitaro manyave namo vaḥ pitaraḥ pitaro namo vo va gṛhānnaḥ pitaro datta sato vaḥ pitaro deṣmaitad vaḥ pitaro vāsaḥ ॥

Since the manes do not make their appearance to accept these offerings, they should be kept either on the roof or in a field; if for any reason this is not done let a hungry guest be fed on them.

Tarpaṇa*

Put on rings of kuśa blades on the ring fingers and thumbs of both hands and, while doing so, read the following mantras:

ॐ पवित्रेस्थो वैष्णव्यौ सवितुर्वः प्रसव उत्पुनाम्यच्छिद्रेण पवित्रेण सूर्यस्य रश्मिभिः। देवीरापोअग्रेगुवो अग्रेपुवोऽग्रे इममद्य यज्ञं नयताग्रे यज्ञपति ७ सुधातुं यज्ञपतिं देवयुवम् ॥

* Refreshing (especially of gods and deceased ancestors by presenting to them libations of water); a particular ceremony performed with a magical mantra.

om pavitrestho vaiṣṇavyau saviturvaḥ prasava utpunāmyacchidreṇa pavitreṇa sūryasya raśmibhiḥ I devīrāpo agreguvo agrepuvo'gre imamadya yajñaṁ nayatāgre yajñapatiṁ sudhātuṁ yajñapatiṁ devayuvam II

This mantra should also be repeated while performing the tarpaṇa. Let the palms of the hands be joined to form a hollow cup and for the offering of tarpaṇa take a little water along with barley, sesamum, rice, milk and flowers.

Deva-tarpaṇa

For offering the libations of water to the deities, drop water with the tip of the kuśa blades as you sit facing the east. Offer the libations of water in front with kuśa blades kept in the hollow of your palms. While making the offering of water with your face towards the east read the following mantras:

ॐ ब्रह्मा तृप्यताम् । ॐ विष्णुस्तृप्यताम् । ॐ रूद्रस्तृप्यताम् ।
ॐ प्रजापतिस्तृप्यताम् । ॐ देवास्तृप्यन्ताम् । ॐ छन्दांसि तृप्यन्ताम् ।
ॐ वेदास्तृप्यन्ताम् । ॐ ऋषयस्तृप्यन्ताम् । ॐ आचार्यास्तृप्यन्ताम् ।
ॐ गन्धर्वास्तृप्यन्ताम् । ॐ देव्यस्तृप्यन्ताम् । ॐ अप्सरसस्तृप्यन्ताम् ।
ॐ देवानुगास्तृप्यन्ताम् । ॐ नागास्तृप्यन्ताम् । ॐ तक्षास्तृप्यन्ताम् ।
ॐ पर्वतास्तृप्यन्ताम् । ॐ सागरास्तृप्यन्ताम् । ॐ सरितस्तृप्यन्ताम् ।
ॐ मनुष्यास्तृप्यन्ताम् । ॐ रक्षांसि तृप्यन्ताम् । ॐ पिशाचास्तृप्यन्ताम् ।
ॐ सुपर्णास्तृप्यन्ताम् । ॐ भूतानि तृप्यन्ताम् । ॐ पशवस्तृप्यन्ताम् ।
ॐ संवत्सराः सावयावास्तृप्यन्ताम् । ॐ वनस्पतयस्तृप्यन्ताम् ।
ॐ औषधयस्तृप्यन्ताम् । ॐ भूतग्रामश्चतुर्विधस्तृप्यन्ताम् ॥

om brahmā tṛpyatām I om viṣṇustṛpyatām I om rudrastṛpyatām I om prajāpatistṛpyatām I om devāstṛpyantām I om chandāṁsi tṛpyantām I om vedāstṛpyantām I om ṛṣayastṛpyantām I om ācāryāstṛpyantām I om gandharvāstṛpyantām I om devyastṛpyantām I om apsarasastṛpyantām I om devānugāstṛpyantām I om nāgāstṛ-

pyantām I om takṣāstṛpyantām I oṃ parvatāstṛpyantām I om sāgarāstṛpyantām I om saritastṛpyantām I om manuṣyāstṛpyantām I om rakṣāṁsi tṛpyantām I om piśācāstṛpyantām I om suparṇāstṛpyantām I om bhūtāni tṛpyantām I om paśavastṛpyantām I om saṁvatsarāḥ sāvayāvāstṛpyantām I om vanaspatayastṛpyantām I om auṣadhayastṛpyantām I om bhūtagrāmaścaturvidhastṛpyatām II

Ṛṣi-tarpaṇa

While offering libations to the seers, continue to maintain the same posture and read thus:

ॐ मरीचिस्तृप्यताम् । ॐ अत्रिस्तृप्यताम् । ॐ अङ्गिरास्तृप्यताम् । ॐ पुलस्त्यस्तृप्यताम् । ॐ पुलहस्तृप्यताम् । ॐ क्रतुस्तृप्यताम् । ॐ वसिष्ठस्तृप्यताम् । प्रचेतास्तृप्यताम् । ॐ भृगुस्तृप्यताम् । ॐ नारदस्तृप्यताम् ॥

om maricistṛpyatām I om atristṛpyatām I om aṅgirāstṛpyatām I om pulastyastṛpyatām I om pulahastṛpyatām I om kratustṛpyatām I om vasiṣṭhastṛpyatām I om pracetāstṛpyatām I om bhṛgustṛpyatām I om nāradastṛpyatām II

The next three libations are those offered to the great seers, manes and the god of death called Yama. Such seers as Sanaka who are deemed divine are also offered libations with the middle of kuśa blades, the performer facing the north and offering two cupfuls of libations with his joined palms. It would be advisable to wrap the sacred thread around the neck like a garland. Read the following mantra as you drop water with the middle of the kuśa blades. Fill the hollow of your joined palms and drop water from near the root of the little finger of the right hand. This is known as prājāpatya tīrtha or in some other quarters prājāpatya mudrā.

ॐ सनकस्तृप्यताम् । ॐ सनन्दनस्तृप्यताम् । ॐ सनातनस्तृप्यताम् ।

ॐ कपिलस्तृप्यताम् । ॐ आसुरिस्तृप्यताम् । ॐ वोढुस्तृप्यताम् । ॐ पञ्चशिखस्तृप्यताम् ॥

om sanakastṛpyatām I om sanandanastṛpyatām I om sanātanastṛpyatām I om kapilastṛpyatām I om āsuristṛpyatām I om voḍhustṛpyatām I om pañcaśikhastṛpyatām II

The next tarpaṇa called pitṛtarpaṇa is offered with the face looking towards the south. Do it three times with the root and the tips of the kuśas joined together as are the palms, the hollow of which contains the ritual water. The orthodox mode of wearing the sacred string is then reversed, the string lying from the right shoulder to the left side. The right knee should be kept on the ground and water should be poured from near the thumb with the kuśa blades folded twice and kept between the trigger finger and the thumb. This is called pitṛ-tīrtha mudrā. This is also the mode of offering water oblation to the divine manes, principal pitṛs and Yama. The oblation to the divine pitṛs should be made with the following sacred mantras:

ॐ कव्यवाडनलस्तृप्यताम् इदं सतिलं जलम् । तस्मै स्वधा नमः ॥१॥
ॐ सोमस्तृप्यताम्, इदं सतिलं जलम् । तस्मै स्वधा नमः ॥२॥
ॐ यमस्तृप्यताम् इदं सतिलं जलम् । तस्मै स्वधा नमः ॥३॥
ॐ अर्यमा तृप्यताम्, इदं सतिलं जलम् । तस्मै स्वधा नमः ॥४॥
ॐ अग्निष्वात्ताः पितरस्तृप्यन्ताम्, इदं सतिलं जलम् । तेभ्यः स्वधा नमः ॥५॥
ॐ सोमपाः पितरस्तृप्यन्ताम् इदं सतिलं जलम् । तेभ्यः स्वधा नमः ॥६॥
ॐ बर्हिषदः पितरस्तृप्यन्ताम्, इदं सतिलं जलम् । तेभ्यः स्वधा नमः ॥७॥

om kavyavāḍanalastṛpyatām idaṁ satilaṁ jalam I tasmai svadhā namaḥ II1II
om somastṛpyatām, idaṁ satilaṁ jalam I tasmai svadhā namaḥ II2II

om yamastṛpyatām idaṁ satilaṁ jalam । tasmai svadhā namaḥ ॥3॥
om aryamā tṛpyatām, idaṁ satilaṁ jalam । tasmai svadhā namaḥ ॥4॥
om agniṣvāttāḥ pitarastṛpyantām, idam satilaṁ jalam । tebhyaḥ svadhā namaḥ ॥5॥
om somapāḥ pitarastṛpyantām idaṁ satilaṁ jalam । tebhyaḥ svadhā namaḥ ॥6॥
om barhiṣadaḥ pitarastṛpyantām, idaṁ satilaṁ jalam । tebhyaḥ svadhā namaḥ ॥7॥

As for the oblations to Yama the following should be chanted not less than three times:

ॐ यमाय नमः । ॐ धर्मराजाय नमः । ॐ मृत्यवे नमः । ॐ अन्तकाय नमः। ॐ वैवस्वताय नमः । ॐ कालाय नमः। ॐ सर्वभूतक्षयाय नमः । ॐ औदुम्बराय नमः । ॐ दध्नाय नमः । ॐ नीलाय नमः। ॐ परमेष्ठिने नमः। ॐ वृकोदराय नमः । ॐ चित्राय नमः । ॐ चित्रगुप्ताय नमः ॥

om yamāya namaḥ । om dharmarājāya namaḥ । om mṛtyave namaḥ । om antakāya namaḥ । om vaivasvatāya namaḥ । om kālāya namaḥ । om sarvabhūtakṣayāya namaḥ । om audumbarāya namaḥ । om dadhnāya namaḥ । om nīlāya namaḥ । om parameṣṭhine namaḥ । om vṛkodarāya namaḥ । om citrāya namaḥ । om citraguptāya namaḥ ॥

Remember that the oblations to the pitṛs should be presented in what is called pitṛtīrtha mudrā in which the person presenting them mentions his name, lineage, etc. The relevant mantras are as follows:

अस्मत्प्रपितामहः अमुकगोत्रः अमुकशर्मा (वर्मा, गुप्तः) आदित्यरूपस्तृप्यताम्, इदं सतिलं जलम् । तस्मै स्वधा नमः॥
अस्मत्पितामहः अमुकसगोत्रः अमुकशर्मा (वर्मा, गुप्तः) रुद्ररूपस्तृप्यताम्, इदं सतिलं जलम् । तस्मै स्वधा नमः ॥

अस्मत्पिता अमुकसगोत्रः अमुकशर्मा (वर्मा, गुप्त) वसुरूपस्तृप्यताम् इदं सतिलं जलम् । तस्यै स्वधा नमः ॥
अस्मत्प्रपितामही अमुक सगोत्रा अमुकी देवी आदित्यरूपा तृप्यताम् । इदं सतिलं जलम् । तस्यै स्वधा नमः ॥
अस्मत्पितामही अमुकसगोत्रा अमुकी देवी रुद्ररूपा तृप्यताम्, इदं सतिलं जलम् । तस्यै स्वधा नमः ॥
अस्मन्माता अमुकसगोत्रा अमुकी देवी वसुरूपा तृप्यताम्, इदं सतिलं जलम् । तस्यै स्वधा नमः ॥
asmatprapitāmahaḥ amukagotraḥ amukaśarmā (varmā, guptaḥ) ādityarūpastṛpyatām, idaṁ satilaṁ jalam । tasmai svadhā namaḥ ॥
asmatpitāmahaḥ amukasagotraḥ amukaśarmā (varmā, guptaḥ) rudrarūpastṛpyatām, idaṁ satilaṁ jalam । tasmai svadhā namaḥ ॥
asmatpitā amukasagotraḥ amukaśarmā (varmā, guptaḥ) vasurūpastṛpyatām idaṁ satilaṁ jalam । tasmai svadhā namaḥ ॥
asmatprapitāmahī amukasagotrā amukī devī ādityarūpā tṛpyatām । idaṁ satilaṁ jalam । tasyai svadhā namaḥ ॥
asmatpitāmahī amukasagotrā amukī devī rudrarūpā-tṛpyatām, idaṁ satilaṁ jalam । tasyai svadhā namaḥ ॥
asamanmātā amukasagotrā amukī devī vasurūpā tṛpyatām, idaṁ satilaṁ jalam । tasyai svadhā namaḥ ॥

Oblations are also presented to all venerable relatives like a senior brother, a step-mother and a dead spouse, while uttering the mantra the name and relationship of the person receiving the oblation should be mentioned. The main pitṛ should be offered three special oblations with the following mantras:

ॐ उदीतरामवर उत्परास उन्मध्यमाः पितरस्सोम्यासः । असुं य ईयुर वृका ऋतज्ञास्ते नोऽवन्तु पितरो हवेषु ॥१॥
ॐ अङ्गिरसो नः पितरो नवग्वा अथर्वाणो भृगवः सोम्यासः । तेषां वयंꣳसुमतौ यज्ञियानाममपि भद्रे सौमनसे स्याम ॥२॥

ॐ प्रपितामहेभ्यः स्वधायिभ्यः स्वधा नमः। ॐ पितामहेभ्य स्वधायिभ्यः स्वधा नमः । ॐ पितृभ्यः स्वधायिभ्यः स्वधा नमः। अक्षन्पितरोऽमीमदन्त पितरोऽतीतृपन्त पितरः पितरः शुन्धध्वम् ॥३॥

om udītarāmavara utparāsa unmadhyamāḥ pitaras-somyāsaḥ I asuṁ ya īyura vṛkā ṛtajñāste no'vantu pitaro haveṣu II1II

om aṅgiraso naḥ pitaro navagvā atharvāṇo bhṛgavaḥ somyāsaḥ I teṣāṁ vayaṁ sumatau yajñiyānāmamapi bhadre saumanase syāma II2II

om prapitāmahebhyaḥ svadhāyibhyaḥ svadhā namaḥ I om pitāmahebhyaḥ, svadhāyibhyaḥ svadhā namaḥ I om pitṛbhyaḥ svadhāyibhyaḥ svadhā namaḥ I akṣanpitaro'mīmadanta pitaro'tītṛpanta pitaraḥ pitaraḥ śundhadhvam II3II

The piṇḍas (balls of rice, etc.) should be made of barley flour mixed with sesamum, jaggery, clarified butter, and milk. Read the following mantras and offer the piṇḍas in conformity with the injunctions of the law books with a view to propitiating the pitṛs.

ॐ उशन्तस्त्वा नि धीमह्युशन्तः समिधीमहि । उशन्नुशत आवह । पितॄन्हविषे अत्तवे ॥

om uśantastvā nidhīmahyuśantaḥ samidhīmahi I uśannuśata āvaha I pitṝn haviṣe attave II

For the pleasure and peace of the main pitṛ offer thirteen oblations with fire, each with the following mantra:

ॐ आयन्तु नः पितरः सोम्यासोऽग्निष्वात्ताः पथिभिर्देवयानैः । अस्मिन्यज्ञे स्वधया मदन्तोऽधिब्रुवन्तु तेऽवन्त्वस्मान् स्वाहा ॥

om ā yantu naḥ pitaraḥ somyāso'gniṣvāttāḥ pathibhirdevayānaiḥ I asminyajñe svadhayā madanto'dhi bruvantu te'vantvasmān svāhā II

Having done this, bow with humility before the pitṛs as you repeat the following:

ॐ नमो वःपितरो रसाय नमो वः पितरः शोषाय नमो वः पितरो जीवाय नमो वः पितरः स्वधायै नमो वः पितरो घोराय नमो वः पितरो मन्यवे नमो वः पितरः पितरो नमो वो गृहान्नः पितरो दत्त सतो वः पितरो देष्मैतद्वः पितरो वासः ॥

om namo vaḥ pitaro rasāya namo vaḥ pitaraḥ śoṣāya namo vaḥ pitaro jīvāya namo vaḥ pitaraḥ svadhāyai namo vaḥ pitaro ghorāya namo vaḥ pitaro manyave namo vaḥ pitaraḥ pitaro namo vo gṛhānnaḥ pitaro datta sato vaḥ pitaro deṣmaitadvaḥ pitaro vāsaḥ ॥

These rituals—not just formalities—having come to an end, one should not forget that there is still a mantra or two to be repeated before the ceremony comes to a successful close. One of the magical texts which should be thought of and repeated now relates to the performer's wish for peace and happiness, for which he must remember the following:

ꣳ ॐ द्यौः शान्तिरन्तरिक्ष ꣳ शान्तिः पृथिवी शान्तिरापः शान्तिरोषधयः शान्तिः। वनस्पतयः शान्तिर्विश्वेदेवाः शान्तिर्ब्रह्म शान्तिः सर्व ꣳ शान्तिः शान्तिरेव शान्तिः सा मा शान्तिरेधि ॥

om dyauḥ śāntirantarikṣaṁ śāntiḥ pṛthivī śāntirāpaḥ śāntiroṣadhayaḥ śāntiḥ । vanaspatayaḥ śāntirviśvedevāḥ śāntirbrahma śāntiḥ sarvaṁ śāntiḥ śāntireva śāntiḥ sā mā śāntiredhi ॥

All scholars and learned ācāryas do not tire of saying that whatever is ordained by tradition and family customs must be religiously adhered to and performed. Generally speaking, the host should, in the first instance, purify himself (perform all the purificatory rites) and then after providing meals to no less than twelve or thirteen brāhmaṇas, offer them gifts and sacrificial fees, bed, etc. in accordance with the prevailing custom. On the completion of these rituals, the performer of the rites should pay a visit to the nearby temple and seek God's blessings. Such moments when the seeker of peace stands before the divine symbol, image or idol, should evoke a mantra like the following:

शान्ताकारं भुजगशयनं पद्मनाभं सुरेशम् ।
विश्वाधारं गगनसदृशं मेघवर्णं शुभाङ्गम् ॥
लक्ष्मीकान्तं कमलनयनं योगिभिर्ध्यानगम्यम् ।
वन्दे विष्णुं भवभयहरं सर्वलोकैकनाथम् ॥

śāntākāraṁ bhujagaśayanaṁ padmanābhaṁ sureśam ।
viśvādhāraṁ gaganasadṛśaṁ meghavarṇaṁ śubhāṅgam ॥
lakṣmīkāntaṁ kamalanayanaṁ yogibhirdhyānagamyam ।
vande viṣṇuṁ bhavabhayaharaṁ sarvalokaikanātham ॥

Thus ends the last of the Hindu saṁskāras called antyeṣṭi.

APPENDICES

APPENDIX I

The mode of annual śrāddha given in the forty-fifth chapter of the *Garuḍa Purāṇa* provides some additional information about the procedure for performing it. The seer bases some of his observations on the institutes of Manu. The relevant portion of what he says about the annual śrāddha is given below:

O Foremost among birds, I shall now tell you the mode of annual śrāddha. Either the kṣetraja of the aurasa son should perform the annual śrāddha in the manner as he performs the pārvaṇa śrāddha. The other sons should perform ekoddiṣṭa and not pārvaṇa. If the father or the kṣetraja and aurasa sons do not maintain fire, they should not perform ekoddiṣṭa but should do pārvaṇa every year or they can perform ekoddiṣṭa also.

If either or both, the son and the father, maintain sacrificial fire, the annual śrāddha should be of pārvaṇa type and the kṣetraja or aurasa son should perform it. But some say whether the dead man does or does not maintain the sacrificial fire, ekoddiṣṭa should be performed on the kṣaya day. If there is kṣaya either at the time of amāvasyā or in the pretapakṣa, the śrāddha should be of pārvaṇa type and can be performed by any son, while ekoddiṣṭa should be done for persons without sons or for women.

If at the time of pārvaṇa śrāddha the performer is defiled by impurity he should perform it on the expiry of impurity. If at the time of ekoddiṣṭa there is any obstacle, the śrāddha should be performed in the next month on the same day. The śrāddha of a śūdra should be performed silently, i.e. without reciting mantras by his wives or sons. The same holds good in the case of a śrāddha of an unmarried girl in a brāhmaṇa family. So says Manu. If two or more die at the same time, the bathing shall be done simultaneously with due mantras but śrāddhas should be performed separately. The śrāddha of the eldest should be performed first and thereafter according to the age. This is the procedure in simultaneous deaths.

He who does all this every year without fail will obtain the best of state having liberated all the manes. If the day of death is not known nor the starting day, only the month is known then *darśa* should be the day for śrāddha. If the month is not known but the day is known then that day may be in Mārgaśīrṣa or in Māgha. If both the day and the month of death are not known then the day and the month when he set out on journey should be taken into count for śrāddha as stated by me before.

Even if the day and the month of starting are not known then those should be the same when the news of his death is received. Even if the month and day are forgotten, when he is not on travel, these should be taken as before. When the householder has gone out of his country and some one dies at home, the period of impurity is over, the śrāddha is on and the householder returns to learn about the sad news, in such a state the householder is not effected by impurity. The śrāddha that has been started by the sons should be finished by them, while the householder shall remain aloof.

If a donor or a receiver does not know of impurity due to birth or death of a relative then no fault accrues. If either of these knows impurity accruing from death or birth of a relative, the fault is of the receiver only, not of the donor of the gift. Whosoever performs the death anniversary of the dead in the above way, liberates him even if the day of death remains unknown to him.

***The Lord said*:**

In the daily śrāddha the brāhmaṇas shall be worshipped,

according to one's capacity, with scents and other things and the manes should be invoked and worshipped.

Āvāhana, svadhākāra, piṇḍa, agnikaraṇa need not be performed. The performer shall observe celibacy during the period. He should worship the Viśvedevas, offer the cooked food to the brāhmaṇas along with the fee. He should pay homage to them as they take leave of him. With the Viśvedevas in view, the brāhmaṇas are fed sumptuously. This rite of feeding the brāhmaṇas is called nityaśrāddha or devaśrāddha.

The śrāddha for the mother is performed first. That for the father on the anniversary day. That for the grandfather on the father's and mother's side on the next day. If he is unable to perform the same on separate days he should perform all the śrāddhas on the same day. The rite of Vaiśvedeva should also be performed similarly. In that case, the offering is made first to the father, then to the mother and then to the maternal grandfather.

In the śrāddha to the mother, if brāhmaṇas are not available, eight noble and chaste ladies whose husbands and sons are alive should be fed. When performing *iṣṭāpūrta,* the procedure is the same. When calamities set in, to ward them off, he should perform a śrāddha in the manner of daily śrāddha. The person performing nitya, daiva and vṛddha śrāddhas as well as the kāmya and naimittika rites in the manner as mentioned before achieves the desired result.

APPENDIX II

Another purāṇa, the *Kūrma,* devotes three chapters (Chapters 20-22, Part II, Vol. 21 of AITM) to the procedure to be followed in the performance of śrāddha. The description is comprehensive and the details testify to the importance this purāṇa attaches to this subject. What is said may be regarded as a representative and typical piece of writing on the subject of śrāddha as the orthodox Hindu looks upon it. The relevant portion of the chapters is reproduced below.

Vyāsa said:

When it is the new moon day, the śrāddha called Piṇḍānvāhāryaka should be devotedly performed by the excellent brāhmaṇas. This bestows worldly pleasures and salvation as its fruit. The śrāddha called Piṇḍānvāhāryaka is recommended when it is the dark half of the month (lit. the moon is on the wane). To the twice-born it is better if it is performed in the afternoon. All other tithis in the dark half of the month beginning from the first, except the fourteenth day, are excellent but the later tithi is more commendable than the former.

The three new-moon days and the eighth day in the dark half of the three months beginning with Pauṣa are good days. The three Aṣṭakās are holy as well as the fifteenth day (the new moon day) in the month of Māgha. Particularly in the rainy season, the trayodaśī (thirteenth day) united with the Maghā constellation is good when the corn is ripe. These are prescribed as suitable for obligatory (nitya) śrāddha.

During the eclipse of the moon and the sun, the naimittika (occasional) śrāddha must be performed extensively among relatives. Otherwise, one is likely to be consigned to hell. The kāmya urged by a desire for benefit śrāddhas are recommended during eclipse etc. and during the vernal and equinotical transit of the sun and during vyatīpāta the last giving infinite merit.

The śrāddha at the time of saṁkrānti (tropical transit of the sun) as well as on birthdays is of everlasting benefit. It is so particularly in all the nakṣatras (constellations) and must be performed at the proper time. By performing the śrāddha in the constellation Kṛttikā the excellent brāhmaṇa attains heaven; by performing it in Rohiṇī, he obtains progeny; by performing it in the Mṛgaśiras constellation, he obtains brāhmaṇical splendour.

By performing the śrāddha in the Ārdrā constellation, one attains the benefits of the holy rites pertaining to Rudra as well as heroism; by performing it in the Punarvasu star, he attains lands, and by performing it in Puṣya he obtains glory and prosperity.

By performing the śrāddha in the Āśleṣā constellation, one attains all desire; in the constellation pertaining to the pitṛs (i.e. Maghā), one attains good fortune. In the constellation to Aryaman (Uttarā Phālgunī) one attains wealth; in the Pūrvā Phālgunī star, the sins are quelled; if the śrāddha is performed in Hasta, one attains excellence among kinsmen; by performing śrāddha in the Citrā constellation, one attains many sons. If śrāddha is performed in Svāti constellation one attains the greatest achievement in trading transactions; by performing śrāddha in the Viśākhā star one obtains gold.

By performing śrāddha in the constellation Anurādhā, one attains many friends; in the constellation Jyeṣṭhā, one attains kingdom; by performing śrāddha in Mūla, one attains flourishing cultivation; by performing śrāddha in Pūrvāṣāḍhā, one attains perfect knowledge and achievement.

By performing śrāddha in Vaiśvadeva (Uttarāṣāḍhā) constellation one attains all desires; in the śravaṇa constellation, one attains excellence; by performing śrāddha in Dhaniṣṭhā one attains all desires; and in Śatabhiṣaj star, one attains the greatest strength.

By performing śrāddha in the Pūrvābhādrapadā constellation, one shall obtain the base metals; in the constellation of Uttarā Bhādrapadā, one attains excellent house; by performing Śrāddha in the Revatī constellation, one attains many cows; and in the constellation Aśvinī one attains horses. If one offers srāddha in the Bharaṇī constellation, one's life becomes perfect.

By performing śrāddha on Sunday, one attains health; on Monday, good fortune; on Tuesday, success everywhere and by performing śrāddha on Wednesday, one attains all desires; by performing śrāddha on Friday, one attains wealth and by performing śrāddha on Saturday, one attains longevity. By performing śrāddha on pratipad (i.e. first day in the lunar fortnight), one attains auspicious sons. On the second day, one begets daughters, and on the third day, one gets animals, on the fourth day, he attains small animals or things and by performing śrāddha on the fifth day, one attains splendid sons.

A person performing śrāddha on the sixth day, attains lustre as well as good cultivation; the man who gives śrāddha on the seventh day, attains wealth; he who offers śrāddha on the eighth day, obtains good trading transactions. He who performs śrāddha on the ninth day, obtains single-hoofed animals; he who performs śrāddha on the tenth day, obtains double-hoofed animals in plenty. One who performs śrāddha on the eleventh day, obtains silver and sons of brāhmaṇical splendour.

One who performs śrāddha on the twelfth day, obtains gold, silver and base metals. One who performs śrāddha on the thirteenth day, obtains excellent kinsmen and one who performs śrāddha on the fourteenth day, obtains ignoble progeny. One who performs śrāddha on the fifteenth day, i.e. on the new moon day, always obtains all desires. Hence śrāddha should not be performed by the twice-borns on the fourteenth day. The śrāddha pertaining to those killed by means of weapons should be assigned to that day.

There is no restriction as to the time, if brāhmaṇas and the materials are available. Hence, the twice-borns should perform śrāddha for the purpose of worldly enjoyment as well as salvation. The śrāddha should be performed at the beginning of all noble enterprises. It should again be performed on the achievement of prosperity, or when a son is born and in similar instances. The pārvaṇa-śrāddha is to be performed on parvans (particular holy days).

The śrāddha that is to be performed every day is the nitya śrāddha; that which is performed for achieving a desirable object is occasional (naimittika). There is ekoddiṣṭa-śrāddha intended for one's forebear and others bahūddiṣṭa (vṛddhi) śrāddha and pārvaṇa-śrāddha. These five kinds of śrāddha are glorified by Manu. In the course of journey, the sixth kind is prescribed and it should be performed assiduously or regularly.

A seventh śrāddha has been enunciated by Brahmā for the achievement of purity. The eighth śrāddha is daivika (divine) by the performance of which, one is liberated from fear. A śrāddha is not to be performed either in the evening or at night except at the time of eclipse. The merit of performing śrāddha at a particular holy place is infinite. The śrāddha on the Gaṅgā, at Prayāga and at Amarkaṅṭaka is of everlasting benefit. The pitṛs sing the religious verse and the learned men dance. "Many sons of good conduct endowed with attributes should be sought by one. Perhaps at least one among all those may go to Gayā. After reaching Gayā if one performs śrāddha incidentally, the pitṛs are redeemed by him. He attains the greatest goal."

In the following holy centres, the pitṛs are perpetually delighted, viz.: Varāha mountain, Gayā in particular, in Vārāṇaśī where Lord Hara himself is present, at the source of Gaṅgā, Prabhāsa, Bilvaka, on the Nīla mountain, Kurukṣetra, Kubjāmra, Bhṛgutuṅga, Mahālaya, Kedāra, Phalgu tīrtha, in the Naimiṣa forest, particularly in Sarasvatī and Puṣkara, in the Narmadā, at Kuśāvarta, Śrīśaila, Bhadrakarṇaka in the Vetravatī, (the Betwa in M.P.) the Viśākhā (Vipāśā, i.e. the Beas), particularly in the Godāvarī and on the banks of the other holy rivers.

One propitiates the pitṛs for a month, if the śrāddha is offered with grains, barleys, pulses, water, fruits and roots, śyāmāka grains, kāśas, nīvāras, priyaṅgus, wheat, gingelly seeds and green gram.

At the time of the śrāddha, one should offer the juice of mango, sugarcane, bunches of grapes and pomegranates. He shall also give *viḍaśvas* and *kuraṇḍas* (different kinds of grass). He should give fried grains with honey, powdered fried grains with sugar, assiduously at the time of the śrāddha. He should give water caltrops and water chestnut (śṛṅgāṭaka kaśerukas).

The following articles are used in the śrāddha, viz.: (long pepper) pippalī, rucaka, musūraka (lentil), kūṣmāṇḍa (pumpkin), alabu (gourd), vārtāka, bhūtṛṇa (a fragrant grass), the juicy root of kusumbha piṇḍa and tandulīyaka. At the time of the śrāddha, an excellent brāhmaṇa should avoid seven articles assiduously, viz.: Rājamāṣa pulse, buffalo's milk, goat's milk, āḍhakīs, kovidāras, pālakīs and maricas (chillis).

On the new moon day, a brāhmaṇa should take his bath and propitiate the pitṛs as mentioned before. With *purity* and gentlemanliness, he should perform the śrāddha called *Piṇḍānvāhāryaka.* At the very outset, he should look up for a brāhmaṇa who is a master of the Vedas. He is the holy centre, deserves to be the recipient of offerings meant for the gods and pitṛs.

The brāhmaṇas to be invited must be soma-imbibers, in yajñas, free from passion (*rajas* quality), knowers of dharma, of calm mind, performing holy rites, observers of rules restraining the mind, those who approach unto their wives only on the prescribed days after menstruation. The brāhmaṇa must be one who maintains the five sacrificial fires. He must be a student of the Vedas, a knower of *Yajurveda,* conversant with many ṛk mantras *Trisauparṇa* and *Trimadhus.* He must know the mantras of *Triṇāciketas,* be a chanter of the *Sāma-veda* and must know the *Jyeṣṭha sāmans.* He must have studied *Atharvaśiras* especially the section called Rudrādhyāya mantras.

He must be devoted to the performance of agnihotra. He must be a scholar knowing nyāyas and the six aṅgas (auxiliary studies of the Veda). He must be a knower of the mantra brāhmaṇas and a reciter of dharma-śāstra. He must be observing vows and sages and a lit. a minor sage, prospective sage of calm mind who has subdued sense-organs. He must belong to family of hereditary Vedic teachers. He must be pure ever since the conception. He must be bestower of a thousand cows.

He must regularly perform the Cāndrāyaṇa rite. He must be truthful in speech, a knower of the purāṇas, devoted to the worship of the preceptor, devas and the fire-god. He must be devoted to the perfect knowledge. One liberated from all sides, of firm mind, an excellent brāhmaṇa who has realised the Brahman, and who is self-possessed, a devotee of Viṣṇu, engaged in the worship of Mahādeva and one called paṅktipāvana (one who sanctifies the row in which he sits for meals).

A person who is as follows, should be known as a paṅktipāvana; one who is engaged in non-violence, one who never accepts monetary gifts; one who performs *satra* (sacrificial sessions) and one who is engaged in charitable gifts.

Brāhmaṇas who are young and healthy and well-versed in śrutis or Vedas, devoted to the performance of great yajñas and those brāhmaṇas who are engaged in the jāpa of the Sāvitrī mantra are paṅktipāvanas. Those who belong to good families, are endowed with Vedic learning, those who are of good conduct, performers of penance, a brāhmaṇa householder who maintains sacrificial fires—these should be known as paṅktipāvanas.

A brāhmaṇa who is engaged in what is beneficial to his parents, who regularly takes his bath early in the morning, a sage knowing spiritual topics and a person of self-control should be known as paṅktipāvana. If the Vedas and vedis (sacrificial platforms) are in disuse up to three generations, that person becomes an evil brāhmaṇa; he never deserves invitation to feeding in śrāddhas, etc. The person mentioned above, a servant of a śūdra, a salaried attendant of the king, the sacrificial priest of śūdras, a person who sustains himself by killing and a person whose livelihood is imprisoning others—these six are brahmabandhus (not true brāhmaṇas—nominal brāhmaṇas).

Manu says that they are fallen for the sake of wealth. These sellers of the Vedas are not approved of for the śrāddha. Those who sell their sons, those who are born as sons of a remarried widow, those who perform the yajñas of even ordinary persons—all these are spoken of as fallen ones. Those teachers who are not cultured, those who read and teach Vedas for salary—are called fallen ones.

That śrāddha wherein the wicked tāmasikas such as old śrāvakas (Buddhists), Jainas, knowers of Pañcarātra, followers of Kāpālika and Pāśupata sects, atheists, and others like them eat food offered to gods, does not bestow excellent benefit here and hereafter. A brāhmaṇa not belonging to any āśrama, or a non-performer of the prescribed duties of his own āśrama stage of life and who falsely poses as belonging to a particular āśrama—all these should be known as defilers of rows of people participating in a feast.

The following persons are shunned in śrāddha and similar rites: a person with a hideous skin; one with ill-formed rotten nails, a leper, one with white leprosy, one with black teeth, one whose penis is mutilated, a thief, an impotent person, an atheist, a drink-addict, a paramour of a śūdra woman, a murderer of a hero, one who indulges in sexual intercourse with one's brother's widow, one who commits arson, a pimp, the seller of soma, the younger brother who marries before the elder brother, the violent man, the elder brother who remains unmarried when the younger brother has married, non-performer of mahā-yajñas, an expelled one, a widow's son, an usurer, a star-gazer, one indulging in songs and musical instruments, a sickly person, a one-eyed fellow, one deficient in any limb, an avakīrṇin (a religious student who breaks his vow), one who has an additional limb, a person who defiles food, bastard, a person accused of a crime, a devala (a person maintaining himself by worshipping idols); a person who injures his friend; a back-biter, a henpecked husband; a person who has abandoned his parents and the preceptor, a wife-forsaker, the creator of discord in one's clan, one who is impure, a worthless fellow; an issueless person, a perjurer, a beggar, a person living by means of dramas, a sea-farer, an ungrateful person, a person committing breach of promise, and one who censures the Vedas, devas and the brāhmaṇas. All these should be avoided in a śrāddha.

The following are defilers of rows: an ungrateful person, a back-biter, a ruthless person, an atheist, a person who censures the Vedas, a person injuring friends and a cheat. All these should not be fed in a śrāddha. They cannot be given any gift in holy rites. A murderer of a brāhmaṇa and a person who is accused should be avoided scrupulously.

A brāhmaṇa who has fattened himself on the food and drink offered by śūdras and a person not performing sandhyā prayers and five great yajñas—are the defilers of the rows in feasts. A brāhmaṇa who destroys what he has learned, one devoid of an ablution and charitable gifts and a brāhmaṇa with predominance of tamas and rajas guṇas—all of these are defilers of rows. Of what use is an expiation beyond limit. Those who do not perform the enjoined duties but perform those acts which are forbidden are to be scrupulously avoided in the śrāddha.

Having purified the ground with cowdung and water on the day previous to that of śrāddha, the performer of śrāddha should invite the brāhmaṇas with the above-mentioned qualifications, through good persons with the invitation: "Tomorrow there will be śrāddha at my place." If this is not possible, he may invite on the next day (i.e. on the day of śrāddha).

Hearing that the time of śrāddha has arrived, his manes will mentally communicate with each other and with the speed of the mind, they gather near him. The pitṛs take food along with those brāhmaṇas, though they themselves are in firmament. They remain in their airy state. After taking food, they attain their greatest goal. The brāhmaṇas who have been invited shall invariably observe celibacy, be self-controlled when the time for the śrāddha has arrived.

The person who performs śrāddha must certainly avoid anger, hurry, carelessness; should speak the truth and have concentration of the mind, refrain from carrying heavy weight, sexual intercourse and long journey. If a brāhmaṇa, invited by one accepts the invitation of another, he falls into the terrible hell and becomes a pig. If the brāhmaṇa householder, after inviting one brāhmaṇa for the śrāddha invites another also out of delusion he is a greater sinner. He is reborn as a worm in the faeces.

If a brāhmaṇa invited for partaking of the śrāddha indulges in sexual intercourse, he incurs the sin of brāhmaṇa slaughter. He is reborn as an animal. If a brāhmaṇa invited for a śrāddha accepts the invitation and goes on a journey, the pitṛs of the wicked brāhmaṇa subsist on sinful food that month.

If a brāhmaṇa, invited for a śrāddha were to quarrel, the pitṛs of that brāhmaṇa become the eaters of filth that month. Hence, the brāhmaṇa invitee for a śrāddha should control himself, be free from anger and devoted to cleanliness. The performer of the srāddha also shall be one who has conquered his sense-organs.

On the morning of the next day (i.e. on the śrāddha day), he should go in the southern direction and with great concentration bring the kuśa grass along with their roots, and he shall place them with their tips to the south and water. They shall be clean. He shall select a clean isolated spot of all auspicious characteristics. It shall be smooth and sloping towards the south. He shall scrub it and smear cowdung over it.

The pitṛs are always delighted with the śrāddha offered in holy centres, on the banks of the rivers, on his plot of land in isolated places but not in waters. One shall never perform śrāddhas in a plot of land belonging to others. What is done by men may be obstructed by the owner out of delusion. Forests, mountains, sacred holy centres and shrines—they say that these are without owners. No one can claim these as theirs.

He shall scatter gingelly seeds there all round, but see that they do not grow (i.e. germinate). A śrāddha affected by the asuras becomes purified through the gingelly seeds if they to not germinate. He shall then prepare various kinds of cooked food with diverse pickles and side dishes. In accordance with his ability, he should prepare lambitives, beverages and cooked food.

Then, after midday, he should approach the brāhmaṇas

who have shaved their hairs and pared their nails and give unto them the tooth-brush twig.

When requested "Ye be seated", they will sit separately. He should give them oil for anointing themselves with as well as water for bath, and various other necessary requisites. These shall be given in vessels made of uduṁbara wood. Everything shall be given with Vaiśvadaivatya rites, i.e. uttering Vaiśvadeva hymns. When they return after taking bath, he should greet them with palms joined in reverence. He should offer them pādya and ācamanīya, (water for washing the feet and the ācamana) sipping water-rite in due order.

The seats of those brāhmaṇas who had been previously invited on behalf of Viśvedevas, are covered with three blades of darbha grass with their tips towards the East. The seats of the brāhmaṇas on behalf of the pitṛs are the darbha grasses facing the south. They must be sprinkled with water and gingelly seeds. He should make them sit on these. Touching the seat he should request: "Ye be seated". They shall sit separately.

Two brāhmaṇas shall represent Viśvedevas. They shall face the east. Three brāhmaṇas represent the pitṛs. They face the north. One shall represent pitāmaha (grandfather) and one shall represent mātāmaha (maternal grandfather) or one brāhmaṇa represents gods and one paternal and maternal grandfather.

Five things are spoiled if performed elaborately in a crowd, viz., hospitality, purity of the place of respect, the time of respect, cleanliness, and the selection of a brāhmaṇa. Hence one shall not wish for elaborateness and a big gathering. Or one shall feed only one brāhmaṇa who is a master of the Vedas, endowed with learning, good conduct etc. and devoid of evil characteristics.

Out of all articles of food thereof, he should take a portion in a vessel and offer it to the brāhmaṇa representing gods, in the shrine, and then pass it to others. He shall consign that cooked food to the fire. He should give that to a brahmacārin. Hence, one shall feed only one brāhmaṇa but he should be an excellent scholar. If a mendicant or a brahmacārin be present for the purpose of food and he seats himself in the śrāddha, one should feed him also.

A śrāddha wherein the guest does not partake of the food, is not praised. Hence, guests should be worshipped in the śrāddhas by the brāhmaṇas. Those twice-born ones who partake of the food in a śrāddha devoid of hospitality to a guest, are reborn as crows. There is no doubt about this. The performer of the śrāddha too is reborn as a crow.

The following shall be shunned and kept at a great distance from śrāddhas, viz. one who is deficient in any limb, a fallen one, a leper, one with running sores, an atheist, a cock, a pig and a dog. One shall avoid a loathsome fellow, an unclean fellow, the naked one, the intoxicated one, the rogue, a woman in her monthly course, the blue-garmented, the ochre-garmented and the heretic. Whatever rite is performed in a śrāddha towards the brāhmaṇas shall be performed along with Vaiśvedeva rites or invoking Viśve-devas.

Even as they are seated, one should bedeck them in ornaments, garlands, coronets, fumigating incenses and unguents. Then with permission of the brāhmaṇas, he should invoke devas by means of the ṛk *Viśvedevāsaḥ* etc. He shall duly recite it and face the north.

He shall wear two pavitras, the darbha grass made to resemble a ring with a tail. Repeating the mantra *śanno devīḥ*, etc. he shall pour water in the cleaned vessel. Repeating the mantra *yavosi* etc. he should place yavas (barley grains) there. Repeating the mantra "yā divyā" he should pour the *arghya* on to the hand. He should then offer scents and garlands, incense etc. according to his ability.

He shall then turn round anticlockwise and face the

south, repeating the ṛk *uśantas tvā* (RV X.16.12) etc. the learned man shall invoke the pitṛs.

After invoking the pitṛs and being permitted by the brāhmaṇas he shall perform the japa of the mantra *āyantu naḥ pitaraḥ* (Vaj. Saṁ 19.58) etc. Repeating the mantra *śanno devīḥ* etc. he should pour water in the vessel and place gingelly seed, repeating the mantra *tilo'si* etc. Pouring arghya on the hands as before, he should, with concentration, put the *saṁsravas* mixing of waters from the argha-vessel and vessel for the pitṛs.

At the seat of the pitṛs, he should place the vessel face downwards. He should take the cooked rice soaked in ghī. Desirous of consigning it into the fire, he shall ask the brāhmaṇas' permission for the same. On being permitted by them saying "Do so", he should perform *homa*, wearing the sacred thread in the usual manner. *Homa* should be performed by one with the kuśa grass in the hand, wearing the sacred thread in the normal manner. All the rites of the pitṛs should be performed with the sacred thread worn over the right shoulder and under the left arm. The Vaiśvedeva rite is performed like *homa*.

While rendering homage to devas, one shall always kneel upon the right knee; and during the obeisance and service to the pitṛs one shall kneel upon the other knee. At the time he should repeat the mantra *somāya vai pitṛmate svadhā namaḥ* (svadhā and obeisance unto Soma the deity with the pitṛs). Then he shall perform homa by saying *agnaye kavyavāhāya svadhā* (svadhā unto Agni, the bearer of kavyas). In case fire is not available one should make use of the right hand of the brāhmaṇas. Or he shall perform it near god Mahādeva or in a cowshed with due concentration.

Thereafter, on being permitted by them he should go to the southern direction. After cleaning and smearing the place with cowdung, he should cover it with sand. It shall be inclined towards the south and be auspicious.

With a darbha grass he shall scratch and scrape its middle thrice. On that spot he should strew darbha grass, the tips of which are turned to the south. With the remainder of the havis he shall make three piṇḍas there and offer them with great concentration.

After placing the piṇḍas he shall wipe off the hand on the darbha grass to remove the greasiness to the pitṛs who partake of the lepa. He should then perform the ācamana rite thrice. He shall smell the cooked rice thrice slowly. The knower of the mantras then shall make obeisance unto the pitṛs. The remainder of the holy water, he should pour round and near the piṇḍas. After offering the piṇḍas he shall smell the piṇḍas with great concentration.

He shall then feed the brāhmaṇas duly with the rice other than that of the piṇḍas. He should also offer them pies, etc. of various kinds, auspiciously prepared in accordance with the śrāddha-kalpa. After they have started taking food, he should strew the cooked rice of the piṇḍas in front of them on the ground. He should ask them "What shall I do with this rice"? When they are satisfied, he should make them perform the ācamana rite. After they have performed the ācamana, he should urge them saying "Be diverted all round". The brāhmaṇas will say then *svadhā be to you.* Then when they have finished taking food, he should inquire of them about the remainder of the food. On being permitted by those brāhmaṇas he shall do so as they say.

In the pitṛ rite one shall say *svaditam* (May it be well tasted). In the cow-sheds it shall be mentioned thus—*suśṛtam* (well-cooked). In prosperity it shall be mentioned thus: *sampannam*—well endowed. In regard to a deva *sevitam* (served) should be mentioned. After bidding farewell to the brāhmaṇas he should stand before the pitṛs silently facing the southern direction. He shall then beg of the pitṛs the following boons: "May the liberal person flourish. May the Vedas and our progeny flourish. May not our faith slip off. May there be much with us for giving."

The piṇḍas may be given to cows, goats, or brāhmaṇas or cast into fire or water. The wife, desirous of a son, may eat the middle piṇḍa. He shall wash his hands and perform ācamana. With the remainder of the foodstuff, he should propitiate kinsmen. He shall give unto the brāhmaṇas whatever is liked by them viz.: cereals, vegetables, fruits, sugarcane, milk, curds, ghī, honey, cooked rice as much as they want and various kinds of edibles and beverages. He should give them various kinds of grains and gingelly seeds of all kinds and different kinds of sugar. Except in the case of fruits, roots and pānakas (sweetened cold water), hot food should be given to the twice-born by one who wishes for welfare.

One shall not rest the knee on the ground nor shall be furious. He shall not utter a falsehood. He shall not touch food with the foot. Nor shall he shun and reject it. The demons take away the benefit of what is partaken of in fury or against the conventional procedure or when served by one who prattles.

One should not stand near if one perspires profusely, he should not see the crows and other birds going contrary to the natural order. The pitṛs desirous of eating, come there assuming those forms. He should not directly give salt into the hand. Nor should the food be served in an iron vessel. It should never be served with carelessness.

What is offered in the following types of vessels yields everlasting benefit viz., golden, silvery, made of udumbara wood or made of horn of rhinoceros. He who feeds brāhmaṇas in mudpots at the time of the śrāddha falls into the terrible hell. He who partakes of the offerings too falls into the hell. One should not discriminate between persons sitting in the same row and serve irregularly. One shall not beg nor force anyone to give. He who begs, who forces anyone to give and who serves with partiality falls into the terrible hells. They should eat the most excellent things prior to others (*vagyatāḥ*) 'observing silence'. But they should not speak out their material good qualities. The pitṛs partake of food only as long as the qualities of the havis are not mentioned.

The brāhmaṇa occupying the seat of priority should not eat it at the very outset. If he eats while many look on, he will incur the sin of all sitting in the row.

One shall read or narrate unto these Vedic passages of self-study, the dharmaśāstras, Itihāsas, purāṇas and the auspicious śrāddhakalpas. Then the partaker of the food should strew the cooked food in front on the ground. He shall ask them *svaditam*? "Well tasted?" If they are satisfied, he should make them perform the ācamana rite. If they have performed the ācamana rite, he should permit them saying "Be diverted". Thereafter, the brāhmaṇas shall say to him—"May svadhā be unto you." When they have partaken of the food he should inform them about remaining cooked food. On being permitted by those brāhmaṇas, he should do as they mention.

In the pitṛ rite, the word *svaditam* is to be mentioned in the *goṣṭha-śrāddha* word, it shall be mentioned thus *suśṛtam*. In *ābhyudayika śrāddha, saṁpannam* is mentioned and in regard to deva, *sevitam* shall be mentioned. After eulogising and bidding farewell to the brāhmaṇas, he should stand silently before the pitṛs facing the southern direction and beg of the pitṛs these boons. "May those charitable donors around flourish. May the Vedas and progeny flourish. May not our faith decrease. May there be much with us to be given." He shall give the piṇḍas to the cows, goats or brāhmaṇas. Or he should consign them to the fire or to the water. The wife who is desirous of a son shall partake of the middle piṇḍa.

He should then wash his hands and perform the ācamana rite. With the food that remains, he shall feed his own servants. Afterwards he himself should take the remaining food along with the womenfolk. One should not remove their leavings before sunset. The husband and wife should observe celibacy on the night. After performing the śrāddha or partaking of it, he who indulges in sexual intercourse falls into the hell Mahāraurava and then attains the birth of a worm.

He should be pure and clean; quiescent and truthful. He should not be furious. He shall have good concentration. The performer and the partaker should avoid self-study and travel. The brāhmaṇas, who partake of another śrāddha immediately after partaking of a śrāddha, are on a par with the great sinners. They fall into many hells. Thus the śrāddhakalpa has been explained briefly but clearly to you. A brāhmaṇa in difficulties shall prosper by performing it.

When he performs Āmaśrāddha (i.e. śrāddha without cooked food) the knower of the procedure endowed with faith should perform the Agnaukaraṇa rite consigning offerings into the fire as well as the offerings of piṇḍas with that alone, i.e. the material used. He whose mind is quiet, who is devoid of sins, and who performs śrāddha in accordance with this procedure shall attain the region of ascetics. Hence, an excellent brāhmaṇa should assiduously perform the śrāddha rite. Thereby the eternal Īśvara would be well-propitiated by him.

An indigent brāhmaṇa may perform śrāddha even with fruits and roots after taking the ablution, with great concentration and performing the pitṛ-tarpaṇa rites with water and gingelly seeds. A person whose father is alive should not perform śrāddha. Some say that he can perform śrāddha to those pitṛs to whom his father offers śrāddha. Or he can perform those rites up to the homa. One can offer śrāddha unto one's father, grandfather and great grandfather. He should offer śrāddha unto him who is his beloved and not to anyone else. One must feed him with devotion who is alive and to his satisfaction. One who is pure and self-controlled does not give unto the dead by transgressing the living one.

Dvyāmuṣyāyaṇika, son of two fathers, i.e. natural as well as father by adoption shall offer śrāddha to both. Similarly a son born of the niyoga rite should perform śrāddha to his progenitor as well as the dead husband of his mother. Then he shall be the true heir. If a son is born out of the semen virile without sanction of niyoga, the son should offer piṇḍas to the progenitor. However, he may perform śrāddha to the kṣetrin (mother's husband). He should prepare two separate piṇḍas to the kṣetrin (mother's husband) and to the bījin (progenitor). He should proclaim the kṣetrin and the bījin in the course of the rite. The ekoddiṣṭa type of śrāddha is to be performed on the anniversary day of the death in accordance with the procedure. When the *aśauca* (impurity) period is over, he can perform any kāmya rite as he pleases.

The ābhyudayika śrāddha should be performed in the forenoon by one who seeks prosperity. All the rites should be performed as though towards devas. No rites should be performed with gingelly seeds. The darbhas shall be made straight. He should feed the brāhmaṇas in even number. As an auspicious beginning, he should recite—"May the pitṛs be pleased." The śrāddha to the mothers should be performed at the outset. That to the pitṛs should be performed thereafter. Thereafter, the śrāddha to the maternal grandfather shall be performed. These three śrāddhas are to be performed when there is a prosperous occasion in the family, such as the birth of a son. This shall be offered along with Vaiśvadeva rite. The anticlockwise circumambulation is not performed.

The scholar should sit facing the east and wear the sacred thread in the normal manner with good concentration and then perform śrāddha. The mothers along with the Gaṇeśvaras should be worshipped at the outset, with devotion, either on the ground coloured in diverse ways or in idols or in brāhmaṇas. One should worship with incense, food offerings and ornaments. A brāhmaṇa should perform the three śrāddhas after worshipping the groups of mātṛs (mothers). If anyone performs śrāddhas without the worship of the mātṛs, they become infuriated and cause injuries.

APPENDIX III

The rituals of Pañcabhūsaṁskāra are as follows:

The host should select the Brāhmaṇa, make him go round the fire and having seated him facing the north, keep the praṇītā vessel before him. Having kept the praṇītā jar to the north of the fire spread four handfuls of kuśa grass around it (the fire) and seize the jar already kept (*prāksaṁstha pātrāsādana*) to the north of the fire. Then have five kuśa blades, three for pavitracchedana and two for purifying and sprinkling ghī, prokṣaṇī jar, vessel with clarified butter, sammārjana kuśa (kuśa for anointing, smearing), upayamana kuśa (a ladle used at sacrifices), three samidhās, sruva, clarified butter, jar filled with rice, etc. May these objects be arranged in the east of the pavitracchedana kuśas in the order stated. All other objects necessary for the Caula should be arranged in the same order as all other objects; the brimful vessel brought at the end, the copper vessel containing some lukewarm water and then another containing cold water, ghī, curd, and butter, a small lump of any of these kept in a jar followed by a ten or twelve aṅgulas long pin which is white at three places in the middle obtained from sāhī,* twenty-seven kuśa blades with pointed tips all ten or twelve aṅgulas long (if possible divided into nine separate bunches of three blades each bound with hand-spun thread), an iron-knife with a copper handle or band, dung obtained from an uncastrated bull and kept in a bronze vessel, and the sacrificial fee for the ācārya. Keep all these in due order. Having done this perform the rest of the

* An animal with a small thorny body.

propitious rites, such as installation of the sacrificial fire* on the altar or in the pit especially dug for it, and all other functions related to it which sanctify an object or a ritual.

The next few steps in the ceremony include taking three chedanakuśas and cutting two of them, each of the span of the thumb and the forefinger. Then with the right hand which has a ring of kuśa grass on it pour the praṇītā water into the prokṣaṇī vessel three times. With the pavitras (two blades of kuśa grass) throw the prokṣaṇī water up into the air. This should be followed by pouring praṇītā water into that contained in the prokṣaṇī three times. The next act is sprinkling water on the butter bowl and keeping the prokṣaṇī right in the middle of the sacrificial fire and praṇītā. This done, pour clarified butter into the butter bowl with another container. Keep the butter on the fire, wave dry kuśas after having ignited them over it (clarified butter) and then throw them into the fire. These ceremonial acts are followed by heating the sruva (wooden ladle) three times and then having brushed them with the root of the kuśas, causing it to be wet with praṇītā water. Repeat a part of this process by heating the sruva three times once again and then keeping it on the ground towards the south of the sacrificial fire. The boiling ghṛta should then be brought down to cool and kept to the north. These sacrificial formalities do not come to an end with this. The householder is advised to keep patience, get up with the upayamana kuśas in his left hand, and with his mind fixed on Prajāpati offer an oblation of three firewoods, all drowned in ghī. This act of throwing the three pieces of firewood should be silently performed one after another without uttering any mantra. Then, taking his seat once again, the householder sprinkles water all

* I.e. kuśakaṇḍikā which usually signifies this. It is placing the sacrificial fire into a special pit or on the altar.

around him while circulating the prokṣaṇī water from the north-east to the end of the north in a circumambulatory order. He should then keep the two kuśa blades (pavitras) into the praṇītā jar and abandon the prokṣaṇī. His next act is to touch the ground with the right knee and after being touched from behind by the Brahmā to offer butter oblations with the sruva to the sacrificial fire. After the oblation has been offered, let him drop with the same kuśa spoon the remaining drops of clarified butter into the prokṣaṇī. Now is the time when he should concentrate on Prajāpati and offer him an oblation by sprinkling clarified butter upon the sacrificial fire. This should be done silently. Offer two oblations of the āghāra, three of the mahāvyāhṛtis, five of the sarvaprāyaścitta and two each of the prājāpatya and sviṣṭkṛt. In this manner offer fourteen oblations altogether and then, having drunk a little potion (saṁsravaprāśana), wash hands, sip a little water, offer the requisite sacrificial fee to the Brāhmaṇa and sprinkle a few drops of water on the head from the praṇītā. The householder should then drop the remaining water in the north-east quarter. His next act should be to mix up the ghṛta with the kuśas and then pick them up one by one and throw them into the fire.

APPENDIX IV*

१. एक दिन छूटि जाय संसार

एक दिन छूटि जाय संसार
. . .(समवेत स्वर)

जिनके ताक पर दीप बरत है ।
जाता वो हाथ पसार ॥
. . .(समवेत स्वर)

राव रंक कोई नाहिं छोड़त ।
सब के करत आहार ॥
. . .(समवेत स्वर)

वेद पुराण ग्रन्थ बहुबिधि पर
कोई ना पावत पार ।
. . .(समवेत स्वर)

भवसागर में जीवन नैय्या ।
राम लगावे पार ॥
. . .(समवेत स्वर)

1. EKA DIN CHUTIJAAYE SANSAAR

Eka din chuuti jaaya sansaar... Chorus

Jin ke taak par dipa barat hai,
Jaataa woe haath pasaar... Chorus

Raava ranka koi naahi chorat,
Sab ke karata aahaar... Chorus

Veda puraan granth bahubidhi par,
Koi naa paawat paar... Chorus

Bhaw saagar me jivan naiyaa,
Raam lagaawe paar.... Chorus

---

* This appendix is specially included for Hindus living in the Caribbean. Courtesy: The Little Store, Trinidad.

२. इतना तो करना स्वामी

इतना तो करना स्वामी,
जब प्राण तन से निकले ।
गोविंद नाम लेकर
मेरी जान तन से निकले ॥

या तो गंगाजी का तट हो,
यमुना का तट निकट हो ।
और सांवरा निकट हो ॥

श्री वृन्दाबन का थल हो ।
विष्णु-चरण का जल हो ।
मुख में तुलसी दल हो ॥

मेरा साँवरा खड़ा हो,
तिरछा चरण धरा हो ।
बंशी का सुर भरा हो ॥

सिर सोहना मुकुट हो,
मुखड़े पे काली लट हो ।
यह ध्यान मेरे घट हो ॥

जब कंठ प्राण आवे
कोई रोग ना सतावे ।
यम त्रास ना दिखावे ॥

इतनी मेरी अरज़ है,
मानो तो क्या हरज्ज है ।
वह आपका फ़रज्ज है ।

2. *ITANAA TO KARANAA SVAAMII*

Itanaa to karanaa svaamii,
Jaba praana tana se nikale
Govinda naama lekara
Merii jaana tana se nikale

Yaa to Gangaajii kaa tata ho,
Yamunaa kaa tata nikata ho
Aura Saavaraa nikata ho

Shri Vrindaabana kaa thala ho
Vishnu-charana kaa jala ho
Mukha men Tulsii dala ho

Meraa Saanvaraa kharaa ho,
Tirachhaa charana dharaa ho
Banshii kaa sura bharaa ho

Sira sohanaa mukuta ho,
Mukhare pe kaalii lata ho
Yaha dhyaana mere ghata ho

Jaba kantha praana aave,
Koii roga naa sataave
Yama traasa naa dikhaave

Itanii merii araza hai,
Maano to kyaa haraza hai
Vaha aapakaa pharaza hai

३. श्री कृष्ण चन्द्र महाराज प्रभु

श्री कृष्ण चन्द्र महाराज प्रभु,
बिनती इतनी सुनिये, सुनिये
... (समवेत स्वर)

जिनके कुछ है अवलम्ब नहीं,
तिनके चरण रखिये, रखिये
इसके अवगुण बहुतेरे हैं,
यहि बार क्षमा करिये, करिये
... (समवेत स्वर)

दीन दयालु पिता तुमही,
निजधाम इसको चाहिए,
मोक्ष दया बिन होत नहीं,
चाहे कोटि प्रबन्ध करिये, करिये
... (समवेत स्वर)

भवसागर धार बहुत गहरी,
कोई नाव वहाँ चाहिए,
सिया राम के नाम का नाव बना,
बिना परिश्रम तरिये, तरिये
... (समवेत स्वर)

ये मृतक जीव की सुधारो गति,
निजदास बन्दा गणिये
कोई भ्रात (?) तुम्हार करै बिनती
दया भगवान करिये, करिये
... (समवेत स्वर)

3. *SRI KRISHNA CHANDRA MAHAARAAJ PRABHU*

Sri Krishna Chandra Mahaaraaj Prabhu,
Binati itani suniye, suniye
...Chorus

Jinake kuchh hai avalambh nahi,
Tinke charana rakhiye, rakhiye,
Isake avagun bahutere hain,
Yahi baar kshamaa kariye, kariye
...Chorus

Diina dayaalu pitaa tumahi,
Nijdhaam isko chaahiye,
Moksha dayaa bina hota nahin,
Chaahe koti prabandha kariye, kariye
...Chorus

Bhawasaagar dhaar bahut gaharii,
Koi naawa wahaan chaahiye,
Siyaa Raam ke naam kaa naaw banaa,
Binaa parisram tariye, tariye
...Chorus

Ye mritak jiiva ki sudhaaro gati,
Nijadaas bandaa ganiye,
Koi bhraat tumhaar karai binati,
Dayaa Bhagavaan kariye, kariye
...Chorus

४. पितु मातु सहायक स्वामी सखा

पितु मातु सहायक स्वामी सखा ।
तुम ही इक नाथ हमारे हो . . . (समवेत स्वर)

जिनके कछु और अधार नहीं ।
तिनके तुम ही रखवारे हो ॥

सब भाँति सदा सुखदायक हो ।
दु:ख दुर्गुण नाशनहारे हो ॥

प्रतिपाल करो सगरे जग को ।
अतिशय करुणा उर धारे हो ॥

भूलि हैं हम हि तुम को तुम तो ।
हमरी सुधि नाहिं विसारे हो ॥

उपकारन को कछु अन्त नहीं ।
छिन ही छिन जो विस्तारे हो ॥

महाराज महा महिमा तुम्हारी ।
समझे विरले बुधिवारे हो ॥

शुभ शांति निकेतन प्रेम निधि ।
मन मंदिर के उजियारे हो ॥

इस जीवन के तुम जीवन हो ।
इन प्राणन के तुम प्यारे हो ।

तुम सो प्रभु पाय प्रताप हरी ।
केहि के अब और सहारे हो ॥

4. PITU MAATU SAHAAYAK SWAAMI SAKHAA

Pitu maatu sahaayak swaami sakhaa,
Tuma hee ik naath hamaare ho... Chorus

Jinke kachhu our adhaar naheen,
Tinke tumhee rakhavaare ho.

Saba bhaanti sadaa sukhdaayak ho,
Dukh durgun naashan haare ho.

Pratipaal karo sagre jag ko,
Atishaya karunaa ur dhaare ho.

Bhuli hain ham hi tum ko tum to,
Hamree sudhi naahin visaare ho.

Upkaaran ko kachhu ant naheen,
Chhin hee chhin jo vistaare ho.

Mahaaraaja mahaa mahimaa tumhaaree,
Samjhe virle budhi vaare ho.

Shubha shaanti niketan prem nidhi,
Man mandir ke ujiyaare ho.

Is jeevan ke tum jeevan ho,
In praanan ke tum pyaare ho.

Tuma so prabhuu paaya prataap haree,
Kehi ke ab aur sahaare ho.

GLOSSARY*

Aṁjali	:	the open hands placed side by side and slightly hollowed; a libation to the manes; when raised to the forehead, a mark of supplication; reverence, salutation.
Agni	:	the fire of sacrifice and the divine Fire, one of the most important gods or divine manifestations, the mediator or priest to men and gods.
Agnihotra	:	daily fire-sacrifice which was performed morning and evening in every household of the higher castes, consisting in an oblation of milk sprinkled on the fire.
Agniṣṭoma	:	Soma sacrifice, lasting for several (usually five) days; one of the most important Vedic sacrifices.
Aham	:	"I", the first person.
Akṣata	:	raw rice grains; unhusked barley-corns.
Amṛta	:	immortal, imperishable; the sacred drink (ambrosia), the nectar of immortality.
Ācamana	:	sipping water from the palm of the hand (before religious ceremonies, before meals) for purification.
Ācārya	:	teacher, guru.
Āditya	:	son of Aditi.

* Only those words are listed here which, besides being technical, have been frequently used in the text or in the rendition.

Ājya	:	clarified butter (ghī) used for oblations, or for pouring into the holy fire at the sacrifice, or for anointing anything sacrificed or offered.
Āhuti	:	calling, invoking; an oblation or offering, especially to a deity; a sacrifice.
Kalaśa	:	sacrificial (festal) vessel.
Kuśa	:	the sacred grass used at certain religious ceremonies.
Gotra	:	a family, race, lineage; a name, appellation.
Candana	:	sandal.
Tṛṇa	:	blade of grass; straw.
Dūrvā	:	bent grass.
Pañcabhūsaṁskāra	:	'ground preparation', a term for five methods of preparing and consecrating the khāra (a quadrangular mound of earth for receiving the sacrificial vessels) at a ceremony.
Pavitra	:	a small sieve or strainer; two kuśa leaves for holding offerings or for sprinkling and purifying ghī.
Prājāpatya	:	relating or sacred to Prajāpati.
Purohita	:	family priest.
Praṇītā pātra	:	the vessel for the holy water.
Prokṣaṇī pātra	:	a vessel for sprinkling water.
Yajña	:	act of worship or devotion; offering; oblation; sacrifice.
Yajamāna	:	the person paying the cost of a sacrifice; the institutor of a sacrifice (who to perform it employs a priest or priests, who are often hereditary functionaries in a family); host.
Vyāhṛti	:	the mystical utterance of the names of the seven worlds (viz. bhūr, bhuvar or bhuvaḥ, svar, mahar, janar, tapas,

		satya), the first three of which, called 'the great vyāhṛtis', are pronounced after *OM* by every Brāhmaṇa in commencing his daily prayers and are personified as the daughters of Sāvitrī and Pṛśni.
Saṁkalpa	:	a solemn vow or determination to perform any ritual observance; definite intention.
Saṁskāra	:	sacraments.
Sruva	:	a wooden ladle shaped like a spoon.
Svadhā	:	the sacrificial offering due to each god, especially the food or libation or refreshing drink offered to the pitṛs or spirits of deceased ancestors. The exclamation or benediction used on presenting (or as a substitute for) the above oblation or libation to the gods or departed ancestors.
Sviṣṭakṛta	:	oblation for the fulfilment of desire.
Havis	:	an oblation or burnt offering; anything offered as an oblation with fire (as clarified butter, milk, soma, grain, etc.)
Havya	:	anything to be offered as an oblation; sacrificial gift or food.
Homa	:	the act of making an oblation to the devas or gods by casting clarified butter into the fire; oblation with fire, burnt offering, any oblation or sacrifice.